THIRD EDITION

SUMMIT 2

WORKBOOK

JOAN SASLOW
ALLEN ASCHER

Summit: English for Today's World   Level 2, Third Edition
Workbook

Pearson, 221 River Street, Hoboken, NJ 07030

Staff credits: The people who made up the Summit team representing editorial, production, design, manufacturing, and marketing are Pietro Alongi, Rhea Banker, Peter Benson, Stephanie Bullard, Jennifer Castro, Tracey Munz Cataldo, Rosa Chapinal, Aerin Csigay, Dave Dickey, Gina DiLillo, Christopher Leonowicz, Laurie Neaman, Alison Pei, Sherri Pemberton, Jennifer Raspiller, Mary Rich, Courtney Steers, Katherine Sullivan, and Paula Van Ells.

Cover credit: Tonis Pan/Shutterstock
Text composition: Electra Graphics

Photo credits: Page 1 (bottom): Dglimages/Fotolia; 1 (center): Martinan/Fotolia; 1 (top): Blanche/Fotolia; 3: Behyar/Shutterstock; 5 (bottom): Nakophotography/Fotolia; 5 (top): Alysta/Shutterstock; 8: Fantisekhojdysz/Shutterstock; 9: Goodluz/Shutterstock; 16: Ollyy/Shutterstock; 21: Neirfy/Fotolia; 23: Kzenon/Shutterstock; 26 (bottom): Innovatedcaptures/123RF; 26 (center): Joggie Botma/Fotolia; 26 (top): Ikonoklast Fotografie/Shutterstock; 28: Szasz Fabian Jozsef/Fotolia; 29: Rido/Fotolia; 31: Boris Spremo/Toronto Star/Getty Images; 33: Marco Secchi/Getty Images Entertainment/Getty Images; 37: Wong Yu Liang/Fotolia; 38 (bottom): Zhu Difeng/Shutterstock; 38 (bottom, center): Minerva Studio/Fotolia; 38 (top): Gstockstudio/Fotolia; 38 (top, center): Jenner/Fotolia; 40: Mrcats/Fotolia; 41: Yuriy Shevtsov/Fotolia; 43 (bottom): Rocketclips/Fotolia; 43 (bottom, center): Monkey Business/Fotolia; 43 (top): Syda Productions/Fotolia; 43 (top, center): Monkey Business/Fotolia; 45: Brainsil/Fotolia; 48: Fisherss/Shutterstock; 50 (bottom, left): Lek Changply/Shutterstock; 50 (bottom, right): Minerva Studio/Fotolia; 50 (top, left): Ramonespelt/Fotolia; 50 (top, right): Oksana Kuzmina/Fotolia; 51: DPA/The Image Works; 52: OLJ Studio/Shutterstock; 55: Pavelkriuchkov/Fotolia; 56: Everett Collection/Shutterstock; 63: Ivan Cholakov/Shutterstock; 65: Monkey Business/Fotolia; 68: Fotolia; 70 (center): Yayoicho/Fotolia; 70 (top): Carlos Santa Maria/Fotolia; 74 (bottom, center): Everett Historical/Shutterstock; 74 (bottom, left): Ksenia Ragozina/Shutterstock; 74 (bottom, right): Dora Zett/Shutterstock; 74 (top, center): Fat Jackey/Shutterstock; 74 (top, left): Livefocus/Shutterstock; 74 (top, right): Cranach/Shutterstock; 77: Tupungato/Fotolia; 79: Nejron Photo/Shutterstock; 82: David Stuart Productions/Shutterstock; 86: Artbalance/Fotolia; 87 (bottom): Kkolosov/Fotolia; 87 (bottom, center): Burlingham/Fotolia; 87 (top): Nicholas Piccillo/Fotolia; 87 (top, center): Pathdoc/Fotolia; 92: Georgios Kollidas/Shutterstock; 93: Pjmorley/Shutterstock; 95: DragonImages/Fotolia; 96 (bottom): Kurhan/Fotolia; 96 (bottom, center): Minerva Studio/Fotolia; 96 (top): Uber Images/Fotolia; 96 (top, center): Sakkmesterke/Fotolia; 097: DPA/SOA/The Image Works; 099: Everett Collection; 102 (bottom): Odua Images/Shutterstock; 102 (top): Daseaford/Fotolia; 103: Everett Collection Historical/Alamy Stock Photo; 108: J. Lekavicius/Shutterstock; 110: Mumindurmaz35/Fotolia; 114 (bottom): Drobot Dean/Fotolia; 114 (bottom, center): Amble Design/Shutterstock; 114 (top): Egyptian Studio/Fotolia; 114 (top, center): Hurricanehank/Shutterstock; 115: Mary Evans Picture Library/Alamy Stock Photo; 117: Dailin/Shutterstock; 118: William STEVENS/Alamy Stock Photo; 119: Blend Images/Alamy Stock Photo; 121: William87/Fotolia.

Illustration Credits: Steve Attoe: pages 4, 56; Stephen Hutchings: page 15; Steve Schulman: page 44; Leanne Franson: pages 14, 17, 20, 53, 57, 58, 65, 101; ElectraGraphics, Inc.: pages 101, 102

Printed in the United States of America

ISBN-10: 0-13-449962-X
ISBN-13: 978-0-13449962-8
1 17

pearsonelt.com/summit3e

Contents

Dreams and Goals

1 Complete the questionnaire.

FIND YOUR DREAM JOB

Do you have your dream job? If not, and you're thinking of changing careers, or if you're just getting started in the working world, this worksheet can help you focus on what you really want to do. Take time to really think about the questions—your answers could determine your future!

1. If you could study any subject, what would it be?

2. What do you think are your strengths?

3. Ask your friends and family for their opinions about you. What do they think are your strengths?

4. If you suddenly had enough money that you didn't have to earn a living, what would you do with your time?

5. What are your hobbies?

6. Do you like working with people? Or do you prefer to work on your own?

7. Do you prefer working outdoors or inside? In an office, or in a setting where you're not tied to a desk?

8. Think about your friends and family. Does anyone have a job that you'd like to have? What is it?

9. What's a job you'd like to do, but you haven't considered it because you don't have the necessary education or training?

Now look at your answers. Do any skills, jobs, or work settings jump out at you? If not, what do your answers have in common? Is there a skill or an area of study that appears often in your answers? At the very least, your answers should give you food for thought about your ideal career.

2 Use each expression in a sentence. Use your own ideas.

a little overkill	keep my fingers crossed
all in all	run of the mill
don't want to take any chances	six of one, half a dozen of the other
I've got my heart set on	wait and see

1. _____

2. _____

3. _____

4. _____

5. _____

6. _____

7. _____

8. _____

3 **WHAT ABOUT YOU?** Answer the questions.

1. Have you ever considered changing your career or course of study? Why or why not?

    _____

2. What job do you see yourself doing in ten years?

    _____

LESSON 1

4 Read the article. Notice the underlined verbs.

The Brooklyn Bridge:
A Story of Triumph

Already an accomplished bridge designer in the mid-1800s, John Roebling <u>wanted</u> to pursue his greatest challenge yet: building a bridge connecting Manhattan with rapidly growing Brooklyn. However, this would be no ordinary bridge. It would span the East River, which flows in more than one direction and can be navigated by ships. The bridge would have to be tall enough for ships to pass under. Roebling's idea was not well received. No one <u>had done</u> anything like it, and experts claimed it was impossible. Many people even doubted the necessity of the bridge.

But Roebling persevered, and he drew up plans for the longest suspension bridge in the world at that time. In 1869 construction began. Roebling <u>had been working</u> on the construction site for only a month when his foot was crushed in a tragic accident. Weeks later he died of complications from the injury. John's son Washington, also an engineer, <u>took over</u>.

Another tragedy soon emphasized the hazards of the project. One stage of construction <u>required</u> workers to go below the river. The effects of the changes in air pressure going from under the river to the surface killed several men and left Washington Roebling paralyzed and unable to speak. But Washington <u>wasn't giving up</u>. He could move one of his fingers a little. He slowly developed a code of communication with his wife Emily by tapping his finger on her arm. With her remarkable assistance, Washington continued to direct the project from his home. Emily took up studies in engineering to better understand Washington's plans. For thirteen years she oversaw work at the construction site.

Even before its opening on May 24, 1883, the bridge <u>had come</u> to symbolize triumph and ingenuity. Today the Brooklyn Bridge remains a tribute to perseverance and determination.

The Brooklyn Bridge connects the boroughs of Manhattan and Brooklyn in New York City.

Now complete the chart. Write the underlined verbs in the correct categories.

Simple past	Past perfect	Past continuous	Past perfect continuous
wanted			

5 **Complete the sentences. Use the correct form of each verb in parentheses.**

1. John Roebling _____ (try) to convince people of his plans
   past perfect continuous

   for the bridge long before the project _____ (become) a reality.
   simple past

2. John _____ (die) before his son Washington _____
   simple past   *simple past*

   (take over) as chief engineer.

3. Construction of the bridge _____ (lead) to tragedies and
   simple past

   triumph in the Roebling family.

4. Emily Roebling _____ (study) engineering while her husband
   past continuous

   Washington _____ (give) orders for her to carry out.
   past continuous

5. Emily _____ (help) Washington for thirteen years before the
   past perfect continuous

   bridge _____ (be) finally complete.
   simple past

6 Circle the action that occurred first in each sentence.

1. (It had been raining for two weeks) when the sun finally came out.

2. He was taking a nap when suddenly the alarm clock woke him up.

3. Marianne decided to take action when she got tired of waiting.

4. By the time I found out the news, everyone had heard about it.

5. Mr. Green was waiting for a phone call when someone knocked on the door.

6. They had sent several messages to the company before they got a response.

7. Nancy had been engaged to someone else when she met Jonathan.

8. When the package finally arrived, they'd been expecting it for three weeks.

9. Jennifer saw the ad when she was looking through the newspaper.

10. I had called the office three times before I finally got hold of someone.

7 Look at the cartoon. Then use appropriate tenses (simple past, past perfect, past continuous, or past perfect continuous) and the verbs in parentheses to complete the sentences. There may be more than one correct answer.

1. Bud _____ (consider) snowboarding down the mountain when Gretchen

   _____ (dare) him to do it.

2. Before Gretchen _____ (say) he should do it, Bud _____ (think) that snowboarding down the mountain was probably a bad idea.

3. Bud _____ (start) to snowboard down the mountain before Gretchen

   _____ (tell) him to stop.

4. When he _____ (hear) Gretchen yell, Bud _____ (get) really nervous.

5. While he _____ (roll) down the mountain, Bud _____ (decided) never to snowboard with Gretchen again.

8 Read the messages on this community website. Then complete the sentences using the phrases from the box.

---

four_corners_community.com

Want to change jobs? Check out our website: Careerchange.com

Ballroom dancing beginners' class (for people with no dance experience)
Tuesdays and Thursdays at 7:00 in the Carter Gymnasium

Chef Wanted 🍽️
The Grand Hotel is looking for a master chef. Training and experience a must. Excellent pay and benefits. Send résumé to Joe.Barker@GrandHotel.com

Having trouble passing your university entrance exams? Not accepted into a program or school? Don't give up! Carlton Test Prep will teach you the exam skills you need to fulfill your dreams. Check us out on the web: carltontestprep.com

Not sure what to do with your life? Talk to a career counselor at FourCornersCareers.com. We can help you make important life choices.

Basic computer classes
6-week course. Our professional instructors will teach you everything you need to know! Morning and evening classes available. ComputersMadeEasy.com

Ballard School of Design is now accepting applications for the fall semester. Submit application and images of your work at Ballarddesign.com

Four Corners Theater Troupe is looking for three actors to join its company for the upcoming season. Prior stage experience a must. Email Emily.Rust@FCTheater.com

---

accepted into	apply to	enroll in	sign up for	take up
apply for	decide on	rejected by	switch to	

1. People who want to _____ art school can _____ Ballard online.

2. People looking for a job as a chef should email Joe Barker in order to _____ a job.

3. People interested in learning basic computer skills can _____ a computer class.

4. Carlton Test Prep might be helpful for people who've been _____ a school or program because of low test scores.

5. The ballroom dancing class is for people who want to _____ dancing.

6. People who want to _____ a different job should look at careerchange.com.

7. People who can't _____ a career can go to the FourCornersCareers site to ask for advice.

8. Only three actors will be _____ the Four Corners Theater Troupe this season.

9 Read the e-mail. Underline the verbs in the present perfect. Circle the verbs in the present perfect continuous.

Dear Mom and Dad,

Well, I've arrived safely, and I'm in my hotel room. I still can't believe I'm here. My dream is finally about to come true! I'm going to skate in the winter Olympic Games! For as long as I can remember I've been dreaming of competing in the Olympics. I've worked so hard for this! I've been training for this day since you took me to my first lesson when I was four years old.

I know you and Dad have given up a lot for me to be here, too. My skating lessons have been expensive, but you have never complained. Everyone has supported me. I know you will all be watching the competition on TV—you've been watching me compete since I first started skating. I hope that I do well so I can make you proud.

Your loving daughter, Tracy

10 Complete the e-mail response from Tracy's mother. Use the present perfect continuous for uncompleted actions, except with stative verbs. Use the present perfect for completed actions.

Dear Tracy,

Your father and I are so proud of you! Since you were a little girl, I ___have known___ that you
(1. know)
would become a great skater one day. You _____ about skating in the Olympics since
(2. talk)
we bought you your first pair of ice skates. I know that sometimes ice skating _____
(3. seem)
like a lot of work. Injuries _____ you slow down a few times, but you _____
(4. make)   (5. not forget)
your goal. And now your dream is finally a reality. We _____ you grow from a child to
(6. watch)
the amazing athlete and beautiful person that you are today. Over the years, we

_____ you win, lose, and try again. No matter what happens in the next two weeks,
(7. see)
we'll be proud of you just like we _____ for so many years.
(8. be)
Love always, Mom

11 Mark grammatically correct sentences with a checkmark. Mark incorrect sentences with an *X*. Rewrite the incorrect sentences using appropriate verb forms.

1. ☒ I've just been enrolling in the pre-med program at the university.

   <u>I've just enrolled in the pre-med program at the university.</u>

2. ☐ I've had an interest in sculpture for many years.

   _____

3. ☐ Have you been accepted by any schools yet?

   _____

4. ☐ How many jobs has he been applying for?

   _____

5. ☐ My daughter's been visiting a lot of universities lately.

   _____

6. ☐ Have you ever been thinking of a career change?

   _____

7. ☐ The group has been working on the project for over a year.

   _____

8. ☐ I haven't been deciding on a career yet.

   _____

9. ☐ I've been owning my car for a year now.

   _____

10. ☐ We've thought about moving, but we really like our neighborhood.

    _____

11. ☐ The International Red Cross has helped people all over the world.

    _____

12. ☐ I've traveled around Italy for the past few months, and I'm loving every minute of it.

    _____

12 **WHAT ABOUT YOU?** Complete the questions with the present perfect or present perfect continuous. Then answer the questions.

1. What is one accomplishment that you _____ (achieve) in the past?

   _____

2. What is one activity that you _____ (do) for a few years?

   _____

3. What is one thing or activity that you _____ (be) interested in for a long time?

   _____

4. What's one thing that you _____ (try) to do for a while?

   _____

5. What's one important lesson that you _____ (learn) in your life?

   _____

13 Complete the paragraph using the words from the box.

ambitious	fulfill	put off	unrealistic
achievable	pursuing	set a goal	

When I was 11 years old, I went snorkeling in the ocean for the first time. That was when I knew that I wanted to be a marine biologist. It was a(n) _____ goal for an 11-year-old, but I knew

1.
that it was _____ if I worked hard. Since then, I've been

2.
_____ my dream. In high school I took as many science

3.
classes as I could. I studied hard and got good grades. It helped that I enjoyed what I was studying. My parents didn't make a lot of money, but I knew it wasn't _____ to think I could get a scholarship to a good university. I did,

4.
and, in four years, I got my undergraduate degree in marine biology. I had to _____

5.
graduate school for a couple of years, but I got an interesting job as a laboratory assistant, so it wasn't so bad. Finally, I was accepted into the graduate program at the university that was my first choice. Now, three years later, I am about to _____ my dream and graduate with my doctorate

6.
in marine biology! Anything is possible if you _____ and work diligently towards

7.
achieving it.

14 Answer the questions.

1. What was one of your childhood dreams? _____
   _____

2. Was that childhood dream realistic? Why or why not? _____
   _____

3. Is it still a dream of yours? If so, what are you doing to pursue your dream? If not, what has changed?
   _____

4. If you live with another family member or a roommate, how do you share responsibilities?
   _____

5. What is something that you've been putting off? Why? _____
   _____

6. Do you think that it's important for children to have one stay-at-home parent? Explain.
   _____

7. What differences do you think there might be between how children with a stay-at-home father are raised and how those with a stay-at-home mother are raised? _____
   _____

15 **Read the article.**

Interviewing for Success

You sent your résumé to several employers, and you got an interview! Congratulations—that's an important step toward landing your dream job. Now you need to prepare for the interview. There's no way to know exactly what questions the interviewer will ask, but there's a good chance that you'll be asked at least some of the questions that follow. Preparing a basic answer to each of them will, first of all, keep you from racking your brain for an answer at the last minute. Even more importantly, it will give you an extra measure of confidence. And a confident candidate is more likely to land the job.

So, let's take a look at some of the typical questions interviewers often ask.

1. Tell me a little bit about yourself.
This seems like a pretty easy question to answer, but you need to give this one some thought and tailor your answer to the job for which you are interviewing. The interviewer doesn't want to know everything about you; he or she is interested in the qualities that will make you the best person for the job. So research the position and prepare a two- to three-minute answer that highlights what it is about you that makes you the best candidate. Remember: this will probably be the first question you are asked, so make your answer a good one so you make a good first impression.

2. Why are you looking for a new job?
This question will almost certainly come up in your interview, so it's best to be prepared for it. If you are a student looking for your first job, the answer is easy. But if you are currently employed, you'll need to explain why you want to leave your current position for a new one. The best thing to do is to highlight the positive aspects of the new job, rather than dwell on any negative aspects of the old job. For example, "I've learned a lot in my current position, but I'm ready for new challenges, which I think I can find at your company." Remember: the key is to avoid being negative about your current job, while telling the truth about why you want to move on.

3. What would you say are your greatest strengths?
This is another question that you will likely be asked, along with its inverse: What is your greatest weakness? Let's start with your strengths. It's hard for many people to talk about their strengths, because it feels like bragging. Start by thinking about which of your strengths and qualifications would be valuable in the position for which you're applying. Those are the ones you want to focus on. Practice talking about them in a way that feels comfortable for you. Remember to provide examples of specific times you have demonstrated each strength.

And now for what might be the harder question:

4. What is your greatest weakness?
You may be thinking, "I don't want to say anything negative about myself; if I do they won't want to hire me." The key when answering this question is to be honest but positive. You should choose a real weakness, but one which you are working to overcome. You want the interviewer to see that you are not afraid to admit that you can improve. For example, "I am not as proficient at [computer programming] as I would like to be, but I have enrolled in an evening training program, and I can see improvement already."

Last but not least, as you're thinking about your answers to these common interview questions, remember to be yourself. Your answers should be truthful and should reflect your qualifications in a way that feels natural to you. Good luck!

Now answer the questions.

1. Why is it important to prepare answers to commonly asked questions before an interview?

   _____

2. When an interviewer asks you to tell him or her about yourself, what type of information should you include? _____

   _____

3. What should you NOT do when explaining why you are looking for a new position?

   _____

4. What problem might some people have when asked about their greatest strengths?

   _____

5. In addition to listing your strengths, what should you do? _____

   _____

6. What should be your goal when answering the question, "What is your greatest weakness?"

   _____

16 **Now imagine that you are interviewing for your dream job. Answer the questions.**

1. Tell me a little bit about yourself. _____

   _____

   _____

2. Why are you looking for a new job? _____

   _____

   _____

3. What are your greatest strengths? _____

   _____

   _____

4. What is your greatest weakness? _____

   _____

   _____

17 **WHAT ABOUT YOU? Complete the sentences.**

1. I have experience _____.
2. I want to get experience in _____ so I can _____.
3. I need to get training in _____ if I want to _____.
4. I have a degree or certificate in _____.
5. I hope to get certified in _____ so I can _____.

   _____

GRAMMAR BOOSTER

A Choose the correct answer to complete each sentence.

1. She _____ to work when her car suddenly started smoking.

   a. would drive   **b.** has driven   **c.** was driving

2. I _____ Turkish food a few times, and I really like it.

   a. used to eat   **b.** have eaten   **c.** was going to

3. We _____ soccer last weekend.

   a. would play   **b.** used to play   **c.** played

4. They _____ vegetables at the market this morning, but it was closed.

   a. would buy   **b.** bought   **c.** were going to buy

5. I _____ you yesterday, but I didn't have time.

   a. had called   **b.** was going to call   **c.** was calling

6. Everyone _____ at the office at 8:30 this morning.

   a. was   **b.** used to be   **c.** has been

7. The workers _____ painting the house before the storm started.

   a. have finished   **b.** used to finish   **c.** had finished

8. I always knew I _____ a house near the beach one day.

   a. would buy   **b.** bought   **c.** had bought

9. Tom _____ meat, but now he doesn't.

   a. was going to eat   **b.** used to eat   **c.** was eating

B Cross out the word or phrase that does <u>not</u> correctly complete each sentence.

1. As a child, Betsy **used to bother / bothered / was bothering** her younger brothers a lot.

2. The team **had been working / used to work / had worked** on the project for months before it was finally finished.

3. I **had walked / walked / was walking** there twice before I learned I could take a bus.

4. The secretary **had left / left / was leaving** a message for Mr. Reynolds on Monday evening before she went home.

5. She thought that she **would see / had seen / had been seeing** that movie by herself.

6. She **used to study / has studied / studied** all the time when she was a student.

7. They **were waiting / had been waiting / waited** for over an hour before their table was ready.

C **WHAT ABOUT YOU?** Answer the questions.

1. What did you do yesterday evening?

   _____

2. What is something that you used to do when you were a child?

   _____

3. What is something that you thought you would have done by the age that you are now?

_____

4. What is something that you've done a few times in the past year?

_____

D Read each sentence. Write <u>C</u> if the sentence is grammatically correct or <u>I</u> if it is incorrect. Fix the incorrect sentences.

           I understand
1. __I__ ~~I'm understand~~ that this is a difficult time for many employees.

2. _____ The secretary remembers that she left the file on Mr. Johnson's desk.

3. _____ Are you having a few minutes to discuss our plans for the project?

4. _____ John is knowing your brother because they went to school together.

5. _____ I'm going to visit my travel agent today. I'm thinking of taking a vacation.

6. _____ This bag is really heavy. How much is it weighing?

7. _____ We're having steak for dinner. Would you like to join us?

8. _____ I'm believing that it's important for family members to live near one another.

9. _____ Mary is looking at photographs of her wedding.

10. _____ This sauce is tasting a little too salty.

E Complete the sentences with the simple present or present continuous form of the verbs in parentheses.

1. **A:** Are these photos of your grandchildren?
   B: Yes. My oldest daughter _____ (have) two sons, and she _____ (have) another one in the spring.

2. **A:** I read that the average newborn baby _____ (weigh) between three and four kilograms.
   B: How heavy is Hannah?
   A: I don't know. The nurse _____ (weigh) her now.

3. **A:** I _____ (see) Julia in the hallway. Want me to get that file from her?
   B: No, don't bother. I _____ (see) her after lunch. We have a meeting at two o'clock.

4. **A:** The food here is delicious. They _____ (have) a lot of great seafood dishes on the menu.
   B: I don't feel like seafood tonight. I _____ (have) a salad.

5. **A:** My parents _____ (think) I watch too much TV.
   B: Mine do, too. They _____ (think) about getting rid of our television.

6. **A:** Did Anne think this sauce _____ (taste) different?
   B: I'm not sure. She _____ (taste) it now.

7. **A:** What are you doing?
   B: I _____ (look) at a photo of my brother's new house. It _____ (look) beautiful!

A   **PREWRITING: TREE DIAGRAM** Look at the tree diagram below. On a separate sheet of paper, create your own tree diagram about your experience, knowledge, training, and abilities. Write ideas in under each section and expand each new idea.

JEFF BROCKMAN

Experience	Knowledge	Training	Abilities
• wrote articles for local newspaper • wrote weekly column for college newspaper • on editorial board of college newspaper	• design newspaper layout with computer software • some Japanese • German	• attended writers' workshop • degree in journalism from Loyalton University	• type 55 words per minute • work well in groups • work independently

B   **WRITING** Most often you will write a cover letter to apply for a specific job. But suppose you wanted to work for the company DreamTECH (or for another real or imaginary company), but did not yet know of a specific job posting. On a separate sheet of paper, write a cover letter to send your résumé to the Director of Human Resources at that company. Use some of your ideas from the idea cluster. Use the cover letter on Student's Book page 12 as a model.

C   **SELF-CHECK**

☐ Does my letter have any spelling, punctuation, or typographical errors?

☐ Did I use formal letter writing conventions?

☐ Did I tell the employer the purpose of my letter?

☐ Did I say why I think I would be a good candidate?

☐ Did I tell the employer how to contact me for follow-up?

Character and Responsibility

1 Answer the questions. Use true information or make up fictitious answers.

1. Have you ever made a serious mistake at work or school? Explain.

_____

_____

_____

2. Did you admit your mistake? Explain.

_____

_____

_____

3. Have you ever forgotten to finish an assignment for work or school? What happened? _____

_____

_____

4. Have you ever broken or lost something you had borrowed? What happened? _____

_____

_____

5. Have you ever broken a promise? Explain.

_____

_____

_____

6. Has anyone ever told you a lie? What did you do?

_____

_____

_____

7. Have you ever told a lie? Did you have a good reason? Explain.

_____

_____

_____

8. Have you ever damaged someone else's car? What happened?

_____

_____

_____

2 Look at the picture. Then write a statement describing the attitude or action of each child. Use phrases from the box. There may be more than one correct answer.

admit making a mistake	express regret	make up for	take responsibility for
avoid taking responsibility for	make up an excuse	shift the blame to	

1. (Charlie) _____
2. (Sally) _____
3. (Billy) _____
4. (Jane) _____
5. (John) _____

3 Complete the conversations with expressions from the box.

couldn't help myself	make it up to	owned up to
let things get out of hand	making fun of	that's not the worst of it

1. **A:** Hello?
   B: Hi Jamie, this is Kelly. I wanted to apologize for _____ your outfit.
   A: Oh Kelly, that's ok. I didn't take it seriously.

2. **A:** What's wrong, Jen?
   B: I messed up big time. I forgot to hand in my final assignment.
   A: Well, the semester just ended. Can you email the professor and ask if you can hand it in today?
   B: But _____. I haven't even finished it!

3. **A:** Who ate all the cake? Billy?
   B: I'm sorry, Mom. I _____. It was so good!
   A: Billy, what am I going to do with you? Well, at least you _____ it and didn't try to shift the blame to the dog!

4. A: Brenda, I'm so sorry I forgot your birthday!

    B: Oh Amy, that's ok. At our age, birthdays aren't such a big deal.

    A: Still, let me _____ you. Can I buy you dinner this week?

    B: Well, you certainly don't need to, but yes, let's go out to dinner. It will be nice to catch up.

5. A: How was the party at the beach last night?

    B: It was great fun. But we may have _____.

    A: What do you mean?

    B: Some people were swimming in the dark. That doesn't seem like a good idea now.

LESSON 1

4 Read the article. Then read each statement and check <u>True</u> or <u>False</u>.

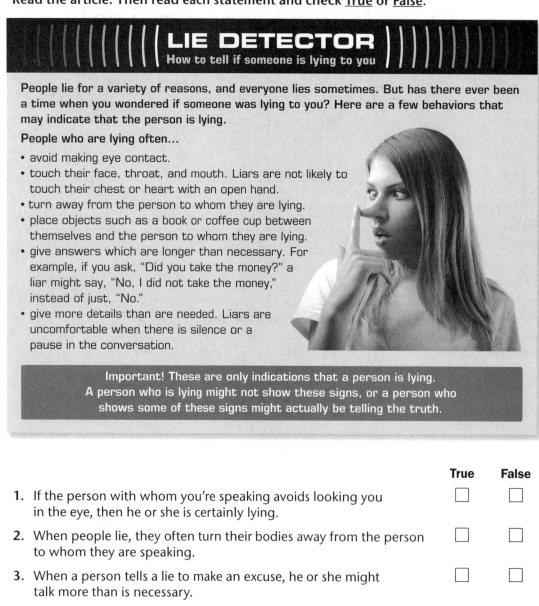

LIE DETECTOR
How to tell if someone is lying to you

People lie for a variety of reasons, and everyone lies sometimes. But has there ever been a time when you wondered if someone was lying to you? Here are a few behaviors that may indicate that the person is lying.

People who are lying often...

- avoid making eye contact.
- touch their face, throat, and mouth. Liars are not likely to touch their chest or heart with an open hand.
- turn away from the person to whom they are lying.
- place objects such as a book or coffee cup between themselves and the person to whom they are lying.
- give answers which are longer than necessary. For example, if you ask, "Did you take the money?" a liar might say, "No, I did not take the money," instead of just, "No."
- give more details than are needed. Liars are uncomfortable when there is silence or a pause in the conversation.

Important! These are only indications that a person is lying. A person who is lying might not show these signs, or a person who shows some of these signs might actually be telling the truth.

	True	False
1. If the person with whom you're speaking avoids looking you in the eye, then he or she is certainly lying.	☐	☐
2. When people lie, they often turn their bodies away from the person to whom they are speaking.	☐	☐
3. When a person tells a lie to make an excuse, he or she might talk more than is necessary.	☐	☐
4. If a person touches his or her chest while talking, then he or she is probably lying.	☐	☐

5 **CHALLENGE** Look at the pictures. Complete each conversation by creating a lie for the second speaker. Then answer each question. Decide whether the person is lying to avoid hurting someone else's feelings or to make an excuse.

1. Why is the girl lying?

   She's making an excuse to avoid being
   punished by her father.

2. Why is the worker lying?

   _____

   _____

3. Why is the boy lying?

   _____

   _____

4. Why is the woman lying?

   _____

   _____

6 **WHAT ABOUT YOU?** What would you say in each situation? Would you lie? Explain your answers.

Situation	Your response
You go to a friend's house for dinner, and he serves fish. He says, "I hope you like seafood." You hate it.	
A co-worker is wearing a new outfit. She asks if you like it. You think it's inappropriate for the office.	
A neighbor who you don't really like invites you to a party. You don't have any plans for that evening but you don't want to go.	
You forgot to do your homework. Your teacher asks why you didn't complete the assignment.	

7 Complete the statements with <u>who</u>, <u>whom</u>, <u>which</u>, <u>when</u>, <u>where</u>, or <u>whose</u>.

1. A liar is someone _____ doesn't tell the truth.

2. There are very few people, if any, _____ never lie.

3. Most people feel at least a little bit uncomfortable _____ they lie.

4. Is there anyone to _____ most people never lie?

5. There are times _____ telling a lie can keep you out of trouble.

6. People _____ lie a lot are often people _____ reputations aren't very good.

7. Lying to avoid hurting someone's feelings is a situation in _____ people often find themselves.

8. Work is one place _____ people sometimes lie to avoid getting in trouble.

"A person who lies
for you will lie
against you."
—Bosnian proverb

8 **WHAT ABOUT YOU?** Complete the statements with your own words and <u>who</u>, <u>whom</u>, <u>that</u>, <u>when</u>, <u>where</u>, or <u>whose</u>.

1. _____ is a person _____ I'd like to meet.

2. _____ is the city _____ I was born.

3. _____ is a holiday _____ many families get together.

4. _____ and _____ are things _____ interest me.

5. _____ is someone _____ ideas I find interesting.

6. _____ is a person with _____ I enjoy spending time.

9 Complete each sentence with a comment clause with <u>which</u>. Use the ideas in the box.

I don't think it's necessary.	I thought it was unfair.
~~I feel awful about it.~~	It was ok, since I was busy anyway.
I find it annoying.	It was very sweet of him.

1. I forgot my aunt's birthday, _which I feel awful about._____ .
2. Jared still hasn't returned the book I lent him last year, _____ .
3. Sarah was half an hour late to our meeting, _____ .
4. Tommy helped his sister clean up her mess, _____ .
5. Stu wants to replace the vase that he broke, _____ .
6. There was material on the test that we hadn't studied in class, _____ .

10 Read the letter to an advice columnist. Then read the columnist's response.

Dear Anita,

I have a friend who frequently asks to borrow things from me. Since she's one of my best friends, I always say yes. But she doesn't take good care of my things. Last month I lent her a book and when she gave it back, the pages were ripped. When I asked her about it, she claimed that the pages were ripped when I loaned it to her, which wasn't true—it was a brand new book! Another time I let her use one of my favorite handbags. I don't know how, but she got a hole in it. That time she said she was sorry, and she admitted that it was her fault. Unfortunately, she still hasn't given me any money for it, which bothers me. Once she borrowed a pair of my shoes, and her dog chewed them. But she said it wasn't her fault—it was her sister's fault because her sister let the dog into her bedroom!

I want to keep my friend, but I can't continue with the way things are going.

Please help!
Christina

Dear Christina,

You sound like a very good and forgiving friend. But it also sounds like you might be a pushover. I know it can be hard to talk openly about a friend's behavior when it bothers you. But it's important. You need to learn to say no, and your friend needs to learn to take responsibility. Next time, before you lend your friend something, tell her that you want it back in the same condition. Tell her you'll expect her to take responsibility for any damage, which is only fair. That way, you explain your expectations and make a plan if she doesn't meet them. Good luck!

Sincerely,
Anita

Now choose the correct answer to complete each statement.

1. Christina's friend doesn't often _____ .
   a. borrow things from Christina
   b. ruin things
   c. take responsibility for her mistakes

2. Christina's friend _____ the ripped pages in the book.
   a. felt awful about
   b. made an excuse about
   c. took responsibility for

3. When Christina's friend damaged the handbag, she _____.
   a. made up an excuse
   b. admitted making a mistake
   c. shifted the blame to someone else

4. After Christina's friend returned the damaged bag, she didn't _____.
   a. make it up to Christina
   b. know about the problem with the bag
   c. admit that the hole in the bag was her fault

5. When the dog ruined Christina's shoes, her friend _____.
   a. shifted the blame to someone else
   b. took responsibility
   c. made it up to Christina

6. Anita thinks that Christina should _____.
   a. express regret
   b. make excuses for her friend
   c. make her friend take responsibility

11 **WHAT ABOUT YOU?** Read the following situation. If you were involved in this situation, would you take responsibility for the accident, avoid responsibility, or shift the blame to someone else? Explain your answer.

You're a college student and, to earn money for school, you have started working a part-time job at a restaurant. On your first day on the job, the manager gives you the keys to the delivery van and asks you to pick up some cakes from a bakery down the street. You have never driven a large van before but, because it's your first day, you are afraid of saying no to your new boss. When driving the van to pick up the cakes, you notice a large, luxury car parked on the street. The car has been parked too far from the sidewalk and sticks out into the street. When you pass the parked car, you accidentally hit it. You stop the van and check the damage, and you notice that the side mirror of the parked car is broken, but that the van has only a few paint scrapes. The street is empty and nobody saw the accident.

_____

_____

_____

_____

_____

12 Read the article.

JOURNAL OF HUMAN BEHAVIOR

The Trolley Problem

Does our behavior reflect our character and our values? Most people would answer yes to this question. Many researchers have studied what people do (or say they would do) when faced with having to choose between two opposing values. One classic dilemma is known as the "Trolley Problem."

Imagine this scenario: You are standing next to a track on which a runaway trolley car is speeding straight toward five people tied to the track. They are sure to die in seconds. However, you can save the five people by simply flipping a switch, which will divert the trolley onto another track, saving the five people. However, there is one person tied to that second track, and he will surely be killed as a result of your action. What do you do?

This ethical dilemma was originally developed in 1967 by moral philosopher Philippa Foot and has been used since then by people studying human ethics, morals, and values. As it turns out, a majority of people would pull the lever and sacrifice the one person, thereby saving the five people. This seems to be a relatively clear mathematical equation for most people: one person's death is outweighed by the fact that five people were saved as a result.

Things get a little more confusing when you add a slightly different scenario to the problem. This version was developed in the 1980s by philosopher Judith Jarvis Thomson. In Thomson's version, you

are again standing near the tracks, the trolley is again hurtling toward the five people tied to the tracks, and they are again certain to die. This time, there is no switch and no second track. However, there is a fat man standing next to the track. If you push the man onto the track, his body will stop the train. He will be killed, but the five people will be saved. Mathematically, this is the same calculation as in the first version of the dilemma. But the difference: the majority of people would NOT push the fat man.

Why the difference? The mathematical equation is the same: five people's lives versus one person's life. Researchers have been trying to solve this question for decades. Studies have shown that when people think about actually pushing someone to his death, areas of the brain that deal with emotion are active. However, when they think about flipping the switch, areas of the brain associated with higher reasoning are active. This may provide some clue as to why the responses to these two similar versions of the dilemma are so markedly different. What do you think?

VOLUME 27, ISSUE 5

Now answer the questions.

1. Restate the two versions of the Trolley Problem in your own words.

_____

_____

_____

_____

2. Do you think the two versions of the problem are morally or ethically different? Explain.

_____

_____

_____

_____

3. Why do you think most people would pull the lever but not push the man?

_____

_____

_____

13 **WHAT ABOUT YOU?** What would you do if faced with the first version of the Trolley Problem? What about the second version? Explain.

_____

_____

_____

_____

LESSON 4

14 **Answer the questions.**

1. Have you ever made donations to causes or charities? Explain.

_____

_____

2. Can you think of a famous (or not so famous) philanthropist? Describe what this person does.

_____

_____

_____

3. Do you know of any well-known humanitarians? What do they do?

_____

_____

_____

4. What is one form of activism that you know about? What is the goal of the activists?

_____

_____

_____

15 **Read the article.**

AN EVERYDAY HERO

Every 56 days, Chip Brady helps save someone's life.

It's not anyone that he knows, and in fact he's probably never even met any of the people he's helped. Chip is a voluntary blood donor. For him, giving blood is a deep, purposeful ritual. It's a chance to express his thankfulness for his own good health, and it's an opportunity to help people in his community. "This is one way that I can truly make a difference in people's lives," he says.

It started when Chip signed up for his company's annual blood drive. He was surprised at how quick and easy the donation was. He also recalls a great sense of contentment and pride at being able to help others. He always knew that giving blood was important, but he didn't expect how great it would make him feel. "Every time I give," he says, "I get this incredible sense of satisfaction because I know that I'm helping someone in the most important way that I can. You never know who might be alive today because of your blood."

Chip admits that sometimes he gets curious about who he's helped. But in the end, he says that he has to be content with just knowing that he's done something good. Chip encourages everyone who can to donate. He wants them to know the joy that comes from helping someone in need.

Now answer the questions.

1. How does Chip Brady make a difference?

   _____

2. Which of the Vocabulary words on Student's Book page 22 would you use to describe Brady? Explain.

   _____

   _____

3. In your own words, explain why Brady donates blood.

   _____

   _____

16 **WHAT ABOUT YOU?** Answer the question.

1. Have you ever helped out a stranger? How?

   _____

2. How do you feel when you help someone?

   _____

GRAMMAR BOOSTER

A **Mark grammatically correct sentences with a checkmark. Mark incorrect sentences with an X. Then correct the incorrect sentences.**

1. ✔ The woman with whom I spoke was very helpful.

2. ☐ The company for whom I worked was very generous.

3. ☐ Now's the time when the truth comes out.

4. ☐ Shirley is a girl that I've known all my life.

5. ☐ The First Avenue Market is one place which I've always gotten fresh fish.

6. ☐ Her ideas are ones what aren't very common.

7. ☐ Is that the teacher which all the students have been talking about?

8. ☐ The palace, whose history can be traced over 500 years, is a historical landmark.

9. ☐ The author who stories won the contest was previously unknown.

B **Complete the sentences. Circle the correct phrase in each pair.**

1. The band has four members, **all of whom / both of whom** were born in Melbourne.

2. The guest brought a cake to dinner, **half of which / some of whom** was later eaten.

3. There are several rumors going around now, **a little of which / none of which** are true.

4. The artist is Alice Flannigan, **most of whom / one of whose** favorite colors is blue.

5. The concert includes the compositions of several local musicians, **a little of whom / a few of whom** have gone on to record their own albums.

6. I've heard two versions of the story, **none of which / neither of which** is very believable.

C **Rewrite each sentence. Reduce the adjective clauses to adjective phrases.**

1. Harry Goldman works for a large company that is located in Osaka.
   Harry Goldman works for a large company located in Osaka.

2. *The Lion, the Witch, and the Wardrobe* was written by C. S. Lewis in 1950.
   _____

3. Those photos, which prove the innocence of the defendant, have been turned over to the police.
   _____

4. People who smoke inside the building may be fined.
   _____

5. Guadeloupe, which is an island territory of France, is located in the Caribbean Sea.
   _____

6. Any student who breaks school rules will be punished.
   _____

7. The file that holds all the documentation of the study was accidentally misplaced.
   _____

A **PREWRITING: USING WH–QUESTIONS** Think about an incident in your life that you regret. Then write Wh–questions about the incident to help generate ideas.

Who _____

What _____

When _____

Where _____

Why _____

How _____

Answer your questions on a separate sheet of paper. Read what you wrote and add other ideas.

B **WRITING** On a separate sheet of paper, describe the experience that you regret, using the answers to your questions. Include details, using adjective clauses when possible.

C **SELF-CHECK**

☐ Did I include at least three adjective clauses?

☐ Did I distinguish between essential and additional information?

☐ Did I use commas correctly in non-restrictive adjective clauses?

WRITING MODEL

When I was sixteen years old, I had a part-time job at an ice cream store. I always worked on weekends. If I wanted to make plans to do something with friends, I had to request time off from work in advance.

One week a band that was one of my favorites was coming to town for a concert. My friends and I bought tickets. We couldn't wait! I requested the night off from work weeks ahead of time. I wanted to be sure that the plans were set.

Then, on the day of the concert I got a call from another girl, Shelly, who worked at the store. She was older than me, and she'd worked there longer than I had. She said a guy who she really liked had asked her out that night, but she was supposed to work. She asked me to go in for her. I said I couldn't because I was going to the concert. She'd have to work or figure something else out.

A little while later my boss called. He said that Shelly was really sick and she couldn't work that night. He asked me to go in instead. I couldn't believe it! She was lying to our boss! I told my boss that I had plans and couldn't do it, but he said that he really needed me and that he was counting on me. I caved in. I went in to work that night, and I missed the concert.

That was a decision which I've always regretted.

Fears, Hardships, and Heroism

1 Read the quotes.

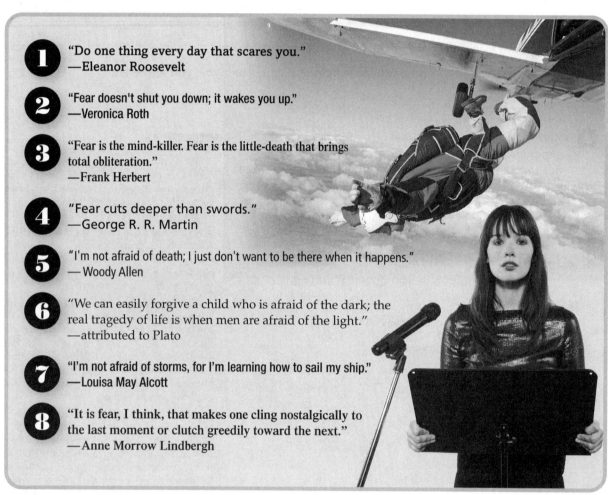

1 "Do one thing every day that scares you."
—Eleanor Roosevelt

2 "Fear doesn't shut you down; it wakes you up."
—Veronica Roth

3 "Fear is the mind-killer. Fear is the little-death that brings total obliteration."
—Frank Herbert

4 "Fear cuts deeper than swords."
—George R. R. Martin

5 "I'm not afraid of death; I just don't want to be there when it happens."
— Woody Allen

6 "We can easily forgive a child who is afraid of the dark; the real tragedy of life is when men are afraid of the light."
—attributed to Plato

7 "I'm not afraid of storms, for I'm learning how to sail my ship."
—Louisa May Alcott

8 "It is fear, I think, that makes one cling nostalgically to the last moment or clutch greedily toward the next."
—Anne Morrow Lindbergh

Now write what you think each quote means.

1. _____

2. _____

3. _____

4. _____

5. _____

6. _____

7. _____

8. _____

2 Pick one of the quotes from Exercise 1 and write about what it means to you. How does it apply to your life and how you approach your fears?

_____

_____

_____

_____

_____

3 Complete the conversations with expressions from the box.

a big deal	it's not the end of the world	take the plunge
be in hot water	jump to that conclusion	with all my heart
freak me out	just chill	you look like you've lost your best friend
got cold feet	mark my words	
have a minor case of the jitters	pulled the rug out from under	

1. **A:** What's wrong? _____.
   B: Oh, I just have a lot on my mind.

2. **A:** Uh-oh. I just broke Mom's tablet.
   B: Uh-oh is right. You're going to _____.

3. **A:** Hi Jane. How did the dance competition go?
   B: I didn't end up competing. I _____.

4. **A:** Wow, my boss really _____ me today.
   B: What happened?

5. **A:** She had promised me a raise, but today she said she couldn't give it to me until next year.
   B: Are you going to look for another job, or _____ until next year?

6. **A:** What's your dream in life?
   B: I want to be an astronaut. It'll be a lot of work, but I want it _____.

7. **A:** Did you buy that car you were looking at?
   B: No, I didn't end up getting it after all. I just couldn't _____.

8. **A:** Lars said he'd call me last night, but I never heard from him. He must not be interested.
   B: I wouldn't _____.

9. **A:** Jenny looked really nervous before her job interview.
   B: I know. I can see why. This interview is _____ for her.

10. **A:** Yikes!
    B: That? It's just a little spider.
    A: I know, but spiders _____.

11. A: Have you heard from that university in California yet?

    B: Yes. I didn't get in.

    A: Well, _____. You'll get into another school.

12. B: I hope so.

    A: _____. You will.

13. A: What's wrong? You look nervous.

    B: I am. I have a big presentation this morning. I _____.

> **Did you know . . .** that it's possible to literally be scared to death? The actual cause of death is a heart attack brought on by sudden, intense stress. And although there are hundreds of documented cases of people actually dying of fright, the statistics aren't as impressive as they might at first seem. Eighty-five to ninety percent of victims had heart disease, and their already weak hearts were pushed beyond their limits by the emotional jolt of fear.

LESSON 1

4 **Choose the best sentence to complete each conversation.**

1. A: That's the third time this week my car has broken down. _____

    B: Looks like it's time for a new car.

       a. I've had it!   **b.** Don't give up!

2. A: Ooh. I really didn't do well on that test.

    B: _____ You'll do better on the next one.

       a. I know what you mean.   **b.** Don't let it get you down.

3. A: How did your interview go?

    B: Not well. I really don't think I'm going to get the job.

    A: _____ I bet the next one will go better.

       a. Hang in there.   **b.** I know what you mean.

4. A: _____ I can't figure out this math problem.

    B: Let me see if I can help.

       a. I give up!   **b.** That must be frustrating!

5. A: I've been taking tennis lessons for a year, but I'm not getting any better.

    B: _____

       a. I know what you mean.   **b.** That must be discouraging.

5 Complete the sentences with <u>no matter</u> + <u>who</u>, <u>what</u>, <u>when</u>, <u>why</u>, <u>where</u>, or <u>how</u>.

1. My grandmother hated to be told she couldn't do something.

   ___*No matter who*___ tried to discourage her, she never gave up her dream of becoming a pilot.

2. Georgia was really frustrated with the last company she worked for. She put in a lot of long hours,

   but _____ hard she worked, her boss never gave her any recognition.

3. That story is completely false. _____ told it to you, there's no way that there's any truth to it. It's only a rumor.

4. There's never a good time to talk to Harry about that. _____ I bring up the subject, he never wants to discuss it.

5. _____ anyone tells her, she's going to do what she wants. She's not taking anyone's advice.

6. Tracy and Jack are still trying to choose a location for their wedding. _____ they decide to have it, I'm sure everything will be gorgeous. They have such great taste.

7. Credit card companies don't care if you have a good reason for making your payment past the due date. _____ you're late, they still charge you a fee.

LESSON 2

6 Complete the statements, using <u>so</u>...(<u>that</u>) or <u>such</u>...(<u>that</u>) and the words in parentheses.

1. The weather was _____ I decided to walk to work. (beautiful)

2. My meal was _____ I ate the whole thing and ordered more. (delicious)

3. That was _____ my ears are still ringing. (a loud concert)

4. The film was _____ I had to leave the movie theater. (scary)

5. She gave _____ no one wanted it to end. (a good speech)

6. Ella performed _____ she has a chance to be on the Olympic team. (well)

7. Your room is _____ you really need to spend the weekend cleaning. (messy)

8. The week went by _____ I feel like we just got here. (quickly)

9. Todd made _____ it was gone within an hour. (fresh lemonade)

7 Complete each statement with <u>so</u> + <u>much</u>, <u>little</u>, <u>many</u>, or <u>few</u>.

1. _____ people signed up for the class that they had to cancel it.

2. There were _____ cars in the parking lot that I couldn't find a place to park.

3. There were _____ storms in the area that our plane had to land in another city.

4. We had _____ time in Montreal that we really didn't get to see much of the city.

5. There are _____ forms to fill out that I'm not sure I'll finish in time.

6. _____ children came to the party that the room was almost empty.

7. I ate _____ lunch that I wasn't hungry for dinner.

8 CHALLENGE Rewrite each sentence, using <u>such</u>...(<u>that</u>).

1. The concert was so good that I didn't want to leave.

   It was <u>such a good concert that I didn't want to leave</u>_____.

2. That blouse is so pretty that I think I'll buy it.

   It's _____.

3. This day was so frustrating that I'm glad it's almost over.

   This was _____.

4. Stu's voicemail was so encouraging that I feel much better.

   Stu left _____.

5. The weather was so bad that we canceled the party.

   It was _____.

9 Answer the questions.

1. People react to fearful situations differently. What physical symptoms are most likely when you are afraid? _____

2. What type of situation might cause you to get butterflies in your stomach? _____

   _____

3. Movies and television programs often show frightening events. Why do you think people want to watch things that scare them? _____

   _____

10 Read the true story about confronting adversity. Then answer the questions.

STORIES THAT INSPIRE · Sign In | Home |

Gender
Female
Male

Age
Under 20
20-40
40-60
60-80
80-100

Location
Africa
Asia
Australia
Europe
North America
South America

Terry Fox: The Marathon of Hope

In 1977 Terry Fox was an athletic teenager growing up near Vancouver, British Columbia. But X-rays taken after Fox felt sharp pains in his right knee revealed unthinkable results: bone cancer. Fox's right leg was amputated 15 centimeters above the knee when he was only eighteen.

But Fox wouldn't be discouraged. Just three weeks after his surgery, he was walking with an artificial leg. He took up sports and running again, and then fostered a new, incredible plan: to run across Canada and raise money for cancer research. He set a goal of $1 for every Canadian. In letters he sent asking for sponsorship, he said: "I'm not saying that this will initiate any kind of definitive answer or cure to cancer, but I believe in miracles. I have to." He called his run "The Marathon of Hope."

On April 12, 1980, Fox splashed his artificial leg in the Atlantic Ocean and began his coast-to-coast run. He ran 42 kilometers a day (the equivalent of a marathon!) through the provinces of Newfoundland, Quebec, and Ontario. News of Fox's journey and the money he collected grew. By the time he reached Toronto, he had attained celebrity status. Crowds lined the streets to watch him pass by, providing a flood of emotional and financial support.

But on September 1, after 143 days, adversity rose again. Cancer had appeared in Fox's lungs, forcing him to stop running. At a press conference announcing the news, he said, "I just wish people would realize that anything's possible if you try. Dreams are made if people try." Inspired by these words, people rallied to collect even more money. By February 1981, $24.17 million had been raised, equal to Canada's population at the time. But while Fox's dream was coming true, he was fighting for his life. The cancer progressed quickly. Canada and the world were devastated when Terry Fox passed away on June 28, 1981, at age 22.

That September, the first Terry Fox Run was held. Over 300,000 people participated, raising $3.5 million. Terry Fox Runs are now held in 60 countries annually, through which more than $360 million has been raised for cancer research.

1. What obstacles did Terry Fox face? Which did he overcome? _____

_____

2. How would you describe Fox's attitude in dealing with adversity? If you were faced with challenges like Fox's, what do you think your attitude would be? _____

_____

3. Do you know someone who has inspired people by overcoming an obstacle? What obstacle did the person overcome? _____

_____

11 **CHALLENGE** Reread the article about Marlee Matlin on page 32 in the Student's Book. Compare Marlee Matlin and Terry Fox. How are they similar? How are they different? Complete the diagram to compare these two people.

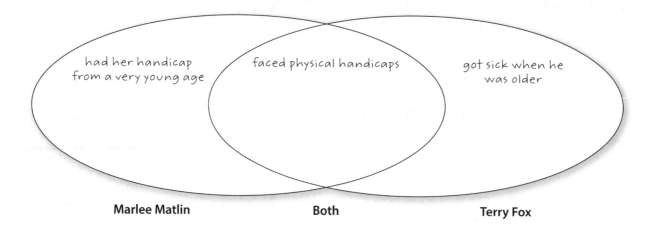

had her handicap from a very young age

faced physical handicaps

got sick when he was older

Marlee Matlin   Both   Terry Fox

LESSON 4

12 Complete the chart with the correct parts of speech.

Adjective	Adverb	Noun
brave	bravely	bravery
willing		
courageous		
	heroically	
	fearlessly	
		confidence

13 Complete the sentences. Use words from the chart in Exercise 12. There may be more than one correct answer.

1. Although Jim has studied French for many years, he lacks _____ in his language ability. He never speaks in class because he's sure that he'll make a lot of mistakes.

2. Tessa _____ jumped in the water to save the little girl who couldn't swim.

3. My neighbor helped a lot of people escape from their houses after the flood. The mayor gave her a medal for her _____ actions.

4. The salespeople at the All-Terrain Sports Shop are always _____ to help their customers. They usually offer to help before you even ask.

5. When the firefighter heard that several children were trapped in their bedrooms, he repeatedly entered the burning house to rescue them. The firefighter was honored for his _____.

6. My two-year-old son isn't afraid of anything—he loves climbing, jumping, and swimming. He even loves snakes and spiders! He's completely _____.

14 Read the profile of Paul Rusesabagina. Then answer the questions.

THE COURAGE AND COMPASSION OF AN ORDINARY MAN

Paul Rusesabagina, a manager of the Hotel Mille Collines in the Rwandan capital of Kigali, did not consider himself an extraordinary man. He was, however, an exceptionally effective businessman, skilled at using his connections with the rich and powerful to keep his hotel running smoothly and to obtain the best of everything for his hotel guests. He knew, for example, that flattering words and gifts of imported liquor and cigars would win him favors from government officials.

Paul Rusesabagina saved the lives of over 1,200 people during the Rwandan genocide of 1994.

But on April 6, 1994, neither Rusesabagina nor most Rwandans could get the only thing that they wanted: safety. On that day, an ethnic group known as the Hutus began killing another ethnic group, the Tutsis. As a Hutu, Rusesabagina was safe. But his wife, a Tutsi, and their three children, were not. With his thoughts focused on his family, Rusesabagina took them to the hotel for safety. He didn't consider taking in other Tutsis or making the hotel a refuge. But as people arrived at the hotel begging for help, he felt he had no choice. Rusesabagina ended up accepting over 1,200 refugees into the hotel.

For 100 days while the killing went on outside, Rusesabagina held off the soldiers from invading the hotel. He used money and luxury goods from the hotel to bribe them. He called in every favor owed to him. When the killing was finally over, Rusesabagina, his family, and most of the refugees had survived.

1. Why do you think Paul Rusesabagina did not consider himself an extraordinary man?

_____

_____

2. According to the profile, what special talents or abilities did Rusesabagina have?

_____

_____

3. Do you think that Rusesabagina's experiences or actions in Rwanda made him a hero? Explain why or why not.

_____

_____

A Combine the two parts of each item to write an embedded question.

1. Why is Jane afraid to fly? (I wonder)

   _____

2. When will our guests arrive? (Do you know)

   _____

3. Where is the office? (Can you tell me)

   _____

4. How far is it to San Francisco? (Would you mind telling me)

   _____

5. How did the pilot land the plane safely in the water? (I don't know)

   _____

6. Is Mary disappointed that she didn't get the job? (Do you think)

   _____

7. Can we stay after class? (Let's ask)

   _____

8. How many people were at the event? (I'd like to know)

   _____

9. Did I turn off the stove? (I can't remember)

   _____

10. Would Dana like to come with us? (Let's ask)

   _____

B Complete each sentence. Circle the correct word.

1. A **cloud / clap / gust** of smoke covered the burning building.
2. There's a **can / box / tube** of detergent for the dishwasher under the sink.
3. Would you mind picking up a **loaf / carton / liter** of bread for dinner?
4. A **clap / bolt / ray** of sunshine cut through the cloudy sky.
5. I'd like a **liter / cup / glass** of coffee with cream and sugar, please.
6. The recipe calls for one **drop / clove / bar** of garlic.
7. A **drop / bar / gust** of wind lifted the kite into the sky.

C Complete each sentence with a phrase from the box. Each phrase will be used more than once.

an act of	a piece of	a sense of	a state of

1. Let me give you _____ advice.

2. After the changes were implemented, many of the employees were in _____ confusion.

3. Mrs. Carson always maintains _____ control in her classroom.

4. The students' refusal to attend classes was _____ defiance.

5. After finally finishing the project, we enjoyed _____ accomplishment.

6. To do this job, it's really helpful to have _____ humor.

7. That's just _____ gossip. I wouldn't pay any attention to it.

8. After standing empty for over 20 years, the old house was in _____ disrepair.

D Choose the correct noun to complete each sentence.

1. There's _____ it will rain tomorrow.

   a. a chance **b.** chance

2. Do you like _____?

   a. a fruit **b.** fruit

3. I've planned everything—I'm not leaving anything to _____.

   a. a chance **b.** chance

4. Did you use _____ on your hair?

   a. a shampoo **b.** shampoo

5. There's _____ on the table. Can you turn it on, please?

   a. a light **b.** light

6. Gold is _____ that is fairly soft.

   a. a metal **b.** metal

7. There's so much _____ coming through the windows.

   a. a light **b.** light

A **PREWRITING: "FREEWRITING" FOR IDEAS**

- Choose a story about a hero. It can be a true or fictional story. It could be about someone you know personally or someone famous. On a separate sheet of paper, write for five to ten minutes all the details about the story you can think of. Write quickly. Do not take time to correct spelling, punctuation, verb forms, time order, etc.

- Then read what you wrote. Choose ideas you would like to develop and put them in logical order.

B **WRITING** On a separate sheet of paper, tell your story. Use adverbial clauses and phrases as well as prepositional time phrases and sequencing words and phrases to narrate past events logically. Use the story about Paul Rusesabagina in Exercise 14 as a model.

Prepositional time phrases
on Fridays
in May
from January to May
at 8:00
by April
during that time

C **SELF-CHECK**

☐ Did I write two or more paragraphs?

☐ Does my report tell the story in the order that the events occurred?

☐ Did I use at least three adverbial clauses or reduced adverbial phrases to clarify time relationships?

Sequencing words and phrases
First,
Next,
Then,
After that,
Finally

Getting Along with Others

1 Read the website.

Sign In | Home |

A Better You

If you're like most people, then there are probably a few things you'd like to change or improve in your life. Check out this list of the most common resolutions that people make. Notice any of yours among them? Click on any that sound familiar for links that'll help you follow through with your good intentions.

Physical Health
Eating
Exercise
Nutrition
Vitamins

Mental Health
Meditation
Stress Reduction
Support Groups
Therapy

- **Spend more time with loved ones.**
  What fun is life if you don't share it with the people you care about most? If you don't have enough time for them, then you've got to make time. They'll appreciate it, and you'll reap the benefits, too.

- **Get in shape.**
  You'll look and feel better if you start taking care of your body. The health benefits of regular exercise are substantial, and maintaining a healthy weight is vital to reducing the risk of illness and increasing longevity.

- **Help others.**
  Whether it's teaching a child to read, volunteering in your community, or building a house, there are so many ways to make a difference in someone's life. Charitable organizations always welcome donations of time, money, and talent.

- **Manage your money.**
  Is money a big source of stress in your life? Whether you want to get out of debt, increase your savings, or just start spending more sensibly, there are lots of ways to get a handle on your finances.

- **Manage your time.**
  Not enough hours in a day to get everything done that you need to? That may be true, but you can still accomplish a lot by simply prioritizing your activities and carefully planning when and how often to do each one.

- **Break a habit.**
  Whether it's smoking, drinking too much coffee, or spending beyond your means, many of us have habits that are self-destructive. Willpower is the key to fighting habits that bring us temporary pleasure but can cause harm in the long run.

Now read the interviews. For each person, choose the resolution on the website that best matches the person's goal or situation.

1. "My goal? That's easy. I want to fit into the suit I wore when I got married. I tried the suit on last week, and I couldn't even button the vest. I've only been married a year and a half! I think every guy thinks he's just a few sit-ups away from a flat, washboard stomach. It was a shock to see how much weight I've gained in such a short time."
—*Jared Strong, Calgary, Canada*

2. "I'm really fortunate that I had the opportunity to receive a good education. I know that there are lots of kids who weren't as lucky as I was, and I'd like to do something to give them a chance to learn. Maybe I could volunteer at a local school as a reading or math coach."
—*Amala Singh, Mumbai, India*

3. "I spent my twenties focused on getting the next big promotion, more responsibility at my job, and a higher salary. Now I look back and realize that my job was my whole life. From now on I want to spend more evenings and weekends with my family and start accepting my friends' invitations to get together."
—*Christobal Valenzuela de Barros, Lima, Peru*

4. "I make a decent salary, but I just can't save up enough money to buy my own home. Everything I earn gets spent on clothes, nice restaurant meals, and movies. I wonder if I'm handling my finances as wisely as I could."
—*Fumiyo Ikeda, Nagoya, Japan*

2 **WHAT ABOUT YOU?** Answer the questions.

1. Do you think any of the resolutions on the website might be helpful to you? Why or why not?

_____

_____

_____

2. Do you ever make resolutions about things in your life that you'd like to change or improve? If so, have you been successful in following through with these goals?

_____

_____

_____

3 **Read the situations. Then identify the shortcoming that each person needs to overcome.**

a perfectionist	controlling	hot-tempered	oversensitive
a procrastinator	disorganized	negative	

1. Tanya spends more time looking for all the things she'll need to do a project than she spends working on the project itself. Nothing is where she thinks she left it or where it should be. She's _____.

2. With the due date for a big assignment quickly approaching, Trevor just can't seem to make himself do it. He'll do anything to avoid it, even clean the house, do the laundry, or go to the gym—activities that he normally hates. Trevor is _____.

3. You can't criticize Pam at all. She gets hurt or angry if you say even the smallest negative thing to her. Even if you're not criticizing her, she takes it the wrong way. Pam is _____.

4. It's not fun to be in the car when Loren is driving. He gets angry at the other drivers over the smallest things. If someone drives too slowly, or turns without signaling, he gets red in the face and starts yelling. It's annoying. Loren is _____.

5. Bruce seems to have a hard time focusing on what's good about a situation. He tends to see the bad things about it, or all of the things that could go wrong. Bruce is _____.

6. Janet needs to be in charge of everything. She can't let her employees make decisions for themselves, even about small things. Janet is _____.

7. David never seems to be happy with his artwork. He's a great painter, but he always sees how he could have made each painting better. David is _____.

4 **WHAT ABOUT YOU? Answer the questions.**

1. Describe a time when you (or someone you know) lost your cool.

_____

_____

2. What kinds of things can set you off?

_____

_____

3. Have you ever told anyone off? Has anyone ever told you off? Explain.

_____

_____

4. Have you ever had to walk on eggshells around someone? Explain.

_____

_____

5. Has anyone ever taken something out on you unfairly? Explain.

_____

_____

5 Write sentences using <u>even if</u> or <u>whether or not</u> and a clause from column 1, combined with a clause from column 2.

1. we had set an alarm

2. you don't mean to criticize Ellen

3. you tell Daniel his work is excellent

4. it's not a big deal

5. I try to be organized

6. I had brought the issue up privately

she still tends to feel hurt

my room still ends up being a mess

we still would have missed the bus

my boss will still make a big issue out of it

he will probably tell you how he'd like to improve it

Jen would probably still have overreacted

1. <u>Even if we had set an alarm, we still would have missed the bus.</u>

2. _____

3. _____

4. _____

5. _____

6. _____

6 Complete the sentences, using <u>only if</u>.

1. <u>Only if</u> _____ you get started now <u>will you</u> _____ have time to finish the job.

2. Tom will succeed in controlling his temper _____ works hard at it.

3. _____ Jennifer gets more organized _____ get a promotion.

4. Your problem will affect your career _____ make a big issue out of it.

5. Tony will do well _____ thinks positively.

6. _____ I write a note to myself _____ remember to run that errand.

CHALLENGE Now rewrite the sentences above, reversing the order of the clauses.

1. <u>You will have time to finish the job only if you get started now.</u>

2. _____

3. _____

4. _____

5. _____

6. _____

7 **Choose the correct word or phrase to complete each sentence.**

1. _____ he apologizes for yelling at me, I won't help him with his project.

   a. Unless   **b.** Only if

2. Can you call me at 6:30 tomorrow morning? _____, I'm afraid I'll sleep in.

   a. Unless   **b.** Otherwise

3. _____ it makes you uncomfortable, I still think you should tell him what's bothering you.

   a. Even if   **b.** Only if

4. We won't make it to the airport on time _____ we leave right now.

   a. unless   **b.** if only

5. Things are going to change, _____ we're ready.

   a. unless   **b.** whether or not

6. Only if you learn to control your temper _____ succeed at this company.

   a. will you   **b.** you will

7. I have to put things away as soon as I'm finished using them. _____, I forget where I left them.

   a. Whether or not   **b.** Otherwise

8. _____ Jack loses his temper easily, he usually calms down pretty quickly.

   a. Even if   **b.** Only if

LESSON 2

8 **Rewrite each sentence as a cleft sentence with <u>What</u>. Use the correct from of <u>be</u>.**

1. I don't understand procrastination.

   <u>What I don't understand is procrastination.</u>

2. I love getting surprised with flowers.

   _____

3. You need a day off.

   _____

4. The dozens of people who visited Eileen at the hospital made her happy.

   _____

5. Seeing so many people at the reception made me grateful.

   _____

6. I didn't expect the many rules and regulations here.

   _____

9 Combine each pair of sentences by writing a cleft sentence with <u>What</u> and a noun clause subject complement.

1. You were late for the presentation. It bothered me.
   What bothered me was that you were late for the presentation.

2. James is so sensitive. It surprises me.

   _____

3. You need to be more organized. That's what she means.

   _____

4. I really appreciated your help yesterday. That's what I was trying to say.

   _____

5. We didn't know anyone at the party. It made us uncomfortable.

   _____

6. You need to be more easygoing. That's what I think.

   _____

10 Rewrite each sentence as a cleft sentence with <u>It</u>.

1. Max made us late.
   It was Max who made us late.

2. Yuki's perfectionism annoys me.

   _____

3. The fact that you forgot your anniversary made her angry.

   _____

4. Karl's negativity bothers his co-workers.

   _____

5. Good friends make all the difference.

   _____

6. The final exam is the most important.

   _____

11 Read about the people. Then summarize the way each person handles anger.
Use expressions from the box. There may be more than one correct answer.

blow one's top	keep it inside	lose one's temper
calm down	let it go	shrug it off
hold it in	let off steam	vent

Because Joe works as a salesperson, he has to be nice to customers all the time, even if they really make him angry. When he gets home after a bad day at work, he sometimes needs to talk to his wife about it. That helps.

Beth found an effective way to control her anger. Whenever she gets mad, she leaves the office and takes a 10-minute walk. When she gets back to the office, she's usually in a much better mood and she's better able to deal with her problem.

After several weeks of being badly treated by his boss, Luis finally got ticked off and yelled at him. Surprisingly, his boss didn't fire him. He actually gave Luis a few days off and began treating him better.

Maggie had a bad day at work today. Several of her clients were rude and yelled at her. But Maggie's pretty easygoing. She just said, "They can get mad if they want to. I'm not going to let it bother me."

1. (Joe) _____

2. (Beth) _____

3. (Luis) _____

4. (Maggie) _____

12 **Read the story.**

There once was a woman who always bought fruit and vegetables from the same local farmer. This farmer had earned a good reputation for the freshness and tastiness of his produce, which he delivered himself in an old truck.

Then, one day, the woman planned a large dinner party. She placed a large order with the farmer to be delivered on the day of the party. However, the day of the party arrived and the farmer did not deliver the goods as promised. Without the necessary ingredients, the woman was unable to cook the wonderful meal that her guests expected. Short of food, she was embarrassed that many of her guests left her party hungry.

The next morning, the farmer appeared at the door carrying the produce that he had promised. The woman, unable to control her anger, yelled at the man, calling him irresponsible and lazy. She threatened to stop buying his products. "What do you have to say for yourself?" the woman demanded.

The farmer answered, "I'm sorry to have inconvenienced you. I didn't make your delivery yesterday because my mother passed away."

Ashamed about the way she had spoken to the man, the woman vowed never to speak in anger again.

Now summarize the lesson that the woman in the story learned about handling anger. Use the Vocabulary from Student's Book page 44 or your own words.

_____

_____

_____

_____

13 **WHAT ABOUT YOU? Complete the sentences in your own way.**

1. When I get ticked off, sometimes I _____.

2. Sometimes I _____ to let off steam.

3. I sometimes lose my temper when _____.

4. When I need to vent I sometimes _____.

14 Read the blog post about friendship.

Getting Along Posted: July 20, 2016

Being There

Just the other day, someone I know in another city posted this on a social networking site: "My paint tray just fell off the ladder. I'm done. I'm just done. I hate everything and I just can't handle moving into this new apartment all by myself." I felt sorry for her, alone in her apartment, with paint all over the place. I could see why it set her off. I commented, "I'm sorry Sara. I know how you must feel." Dozens of other people commented, too. One said, "RATS! I hate when that happens." Another said, "Sorry, Sara. But don't hold on to your negative feelings. Let it go." Maria, who is Sara's neighbor, commented, "I'm coming over NOW!"

💬 **Comment**   ➡ **Share**

Soon after, Maria came over to Sara's place, and let her vent. (Sara talked and yelled for half an hour about how hard things were.) Maria helped her clean up the paint and then finished painting the hallway. Of course, with all that help, Sara was able to calm down.

Sara's experience got me thinking about friendship and social networking. Can a virtual friend be a real friend? This is what I decided. Even if you have a thousand "friends" on a social networking site, it's likely you will have only a few real friends in your life. Here's why.

Can a virtual friend help you clean up the spill?

When something goes wrong in your life, lots of people will sympathize with you and try to make you feel better. Social networking does that very well, and it can be a good thing. Unless you have a friend nearby, though, you probably won't have someone to help you fix things, whether you make a little slip or mess up big time. What I mean is that actually being there to help you pick up the pieces matters. For one thing, friendships are built while we help each other. When someone helps you clean up spilled paint or fix your broken bike, they are showing that you can depend on them. When someone comes to your grandfather's funeral and sits beside you, you are learning that this person truly cares. A virtual friend can cheer you up or give you good advice, but it is the friend who stands next to you who earns your trust.

Can a virtual friend really believe in you?

Most of us have goals in life. Whether or not you are sure you are going to succeed, a friend's belief in you will put the wind beneath your wings. You may post a video of yourself singing online and get a hundred "likes." But when the person shows up at your recital and gives you a vote of confidence in person, you can really feel it. And when someone helps you find new songs, goes shopping with you to look for a recital outfit, and helps you let off steam when you're frustrated, you have a real friend.

Can a virtual friend really know you?

The American writer and historian Henry Adams said, "One friend in a lifetime is much; two are many; three are hardly possible." What Adams is talking about is a very special kind of friend, one who actually knows you. On a social networking site, you choose how you present yourself. What your virtual friends learn about you is entirely up to you. It's not at all the complete picture. But someone who is actually part of your life sees the sorrow even when you try to hold it in and the courage you're too modest to brag about. They also know that you are sometimes too critical and you lose your cool about things that shouldn't really bother you. They know you're not perfect. And they care about you anyway. Only someone who genuinely knows all the parts of you—good and bad—can really accept you as you. That person knows the real you and is, therefore, a true friend. And virtual friends just can't do that.

Now answer the questions.

1. Summarize how the writer defines a "real" friend.

   _____

   _____

2. According to the writer, what are some things real friends do that virtual friends cannot do?

   _____

   _____

3. What does the writer mean when she says that a real friend "earns your trust"?

   _____

   _____

4. Why does the writer feel that online friends can't know the real you?

   _____

   _____

15 **WHAT ABOUT YOU?** Answer the questions.

1. Do you agree with the writer's description of what a friend is? Would you define friendship any differently? How?

   _____

   _____

2. Do you agree that virtual friends cannot be as "real" or as "good" as friends who are part of your daily life? Explain.

   _____

   _____

3. Think about your virtual friends and the friends who are part of your daily life. Do you have any examples to support or refute the writer's opinion? Explain.

   _____

   _____

16 Describe one of your friends. What are this person's strengths? In what ways do you rely on this friend? In what ways does your friend rely on you? Which of the qualities of friendship from Student's Book page 46 apply to your friendship?

   _____

   _____

   _____

   _____

   _____

   _____

GRAMMAR BOOSTER

A   **Complete the sentences. Circle the correct word or phrase.**

1. **Although / As long as / Besides** she drank coffee for over 20 years, my mother has recently switched to green tea.

2. The amount of trash produced in this country has dropped. **Otherwise / Still / In fact,** there are people who throw away things like glass, paper, and aluminum that could be recycled.

3. In my opinion, the high price of those concert tickets is worth it. **That is / Now that / Similarly,** I'd pay $100 to go if tickets were still available.

4. The best ways to lose weight are through a nutritious diet and exercise. **Nonetheless / Whereas / Unless** you change your eating and exercise habits, you'll never get results.

5. Donald Frank is an excellent candidate for the job because of his education. **While / Moreover / As a result,** he has professional experience in the field.

6. Georgia King is very generous with her time. **For instance / Consequently / Furthermore,** last week she volunteered 30 hours at the public library.

B   **Complete each sentence with a conjunction or transition from the box.**

as long as	in other words	nonetheless	so
besides	likewise	now that	whether

1. Charlie did poorly at school but was successful in life. _____, his son James was never a good student but started a very profitable business.

2. _____ we're tested on this information or not, we should still study it. It could be very useful later on.

3. Bob Alderson really dislikes public speaking. _____, he does it frequently for his job.

4. People were stressed out for a while. _____ a decision has been made, everyone is feeling relieved.

5. Clark College appeals to a lot of non-traditional students. _____ night and weekend classes, the school offers several online courses, which allows people to continue to work while they study.

6. _____ Jean Hicks continues at her current pace, she'll easily win the race.

7. Lauren Cook has the best sales record in the company. _____, she's the company's most valuable salesperson.

8. The department head wanted to show his appreciation for the employees' efforts, _____ he took the entire group out to lunch.

C   **Combine each pair of sentences into one sentence. Use the conjunction or transition in parentheses and the correct punctuation.**

1. Harry has only studied Italian for a year. He is the best student in the class. (however)

   Harry has only studied Italian for a year; however, he is the best student in the class.

2. Karen has a good head for numbers. She's very good at chemistry and physics. (furthermore)

3. We're facing a big challenge. We're managing to stay positive. (even though)

_____

4. Sharon is saving money right now. She can buy a house in a few years. (so that)

_____

5. I don't really like vegetables. I eat them because they're good for me. (though)

_____

6. Lucia disliked the ring that her husband gave her on their anniversary. She wore it every day to avoid hurting his feelings. (yet)

_____

D Complete the answers with information about yourself and your friends. Complete each answer with a cleft sentence with <u>What</u>, using the underlined information.

1. <u>Are you looking forward to</u> relaxing this weekend?

Actually, _what I'm looking forward to is going to the gym._____

2. <u>Do your friends like</u> going to concerts?

Actually, _____

3. <u>Does it bother you</u> when someone interrupts you?

Actually, _____

4. <u>Would your friends say</u> that you're oversensitive?

Actually, _____

5. <u>Do you enjoy</u> exercising?

Actually, _____

6. <u>Are you looking forward to</u> spending time with your family this weekend?

Actually, _____

E Restate the answers, using cleft sentences with <u>It</u> to clarify who, what, when, where, or why.

1. **A:** Did they decide to have the meeting in Boston?

   B: (They decided to have it in Houston.) Actually, _it was Houston where they decided to have it_ .

2. **A:** Did you yell at your boss in the meeting today?

   B: (I didn't, but Janie did.) Actually, _____.

3. **A:** Do long meetings really bother Gretchen?

   B: (They don't, but unnecessary meetings do.) No. It's _____.

4. **A:** Is the restaurant usually crowded at 6:00?

   B: (No, but it's crowded from 7 to 8:30.) No, usually _____.

5. **A:** Are you mad because Tammy interrupted you?

   B: (I'm mad because she's always late.) No, _____.

"Don't ask yourself what the world needs—ask yourself what makes you come alive, and then go do that. Because what the world needs is people who have come alive."

—Harold Thurman Whitman, philosopher and theologian

A **PREWRITING: OUTLINING** You are going to write some tips for making a change. Choose one of the changes in the box or think of your own. Write it on the line labeled "Change" and then propose three ways of making the change.

Change: _____

Ways to make the change:

1. _____

2. _____

3. _____

Changes:
- Overcome a shortcoming
- Reduce stress
- Manage anger
- Adopt a new lifestyle
- Your own idea: _____

Example:
Change: *overcome perfectionism*
Ways to make the change:
1. *be less critical of myself when I make mistakes*
2. *learn to accept myself the way I am*
3. *set realistic goals*

B **WRITING** On a separate piece of paper, develop each way listed in Exercise A into a paragraph. Start all three paragraphs with topic sentences. Be sure to use a transitional topic sentence for paragraphs 2 and 3.

Presenting contrasting information
Although
However,
On the other hand, . . .
Even though . . .
Despite the fact that . . .
Nevertheless, . . .

C **SELF-CHECK**

☐ Does the first paragraph have a topic sentence?

☐ Do the paragraphs that follow have transitional topic sentences?

☐ Does each transitional topic sentence clearly link to previous content?

Presenting additional information
Furthermore, . . .
Moreover, . . .
More importantly,

1 Look at the photos.

Do you find any of the photos funny? Why or why not?

_____

_____

2 Answer the questions.

1. Have you ever tried to say something funny, only to have it go over like a lead balloon? Explain.

_____

2. Describe a time when you (or someone you know) made a total fool of yourself. _____

_____

3. What is something that just isn't done in your culture? Why? _____

_____

4. What is something people do that you just don't get? _____

_____

5. What is a piece of advice you've been given that is easier said than done? _____

_____

3 **Answer the questions. Then read the article.**

1. Do you believe that you laugh more or less than most people? Do you believe that there are health benefits to laughter?

_____

2. What could people do to spend more time laughing? _____

_____

Laughter Clubs Make Health a Laughing Matter

Nowadays most doctors agree that laughter provides a number of health benefits. But the challenge is to get people to start laughing.

In 1995, Dr. Madan Kataria, a physician from Mumbai, India, came up with a solution: laughter clubs. He has said that the idea for a laughter club came to him "like a divine light." People join groups for all sorts of motivation, learning, and support. Why not to laugh?

In the first few laughter club meetings, group members took turns telling jokes. But after a few weeks people had a hard time finding new jokes. Some started telling dirty and offensive jokes. So Dr. Kataria revised his idea. He decided that the club members needed to learn to laugh without any jokes or source of humor.

Dr. Kataria developed a method of self-induced laughter, which he called laughter yoga. Explaining a little about the method, he said, "In a nutshell, laughter yoga is a combination of self-induced laughter, yoga exercises, yoga breathing, and stretching exercises."

He advised, "Start with a large group—the bigger, the better." Each laughter club gathering starts with a deep-breathing exercise, followed by chanting the syllables ho-ho-ha-ha-ha. Members then participate in laughter exercises,

Dr. Madan Kataria, founder of laughter yoga

or simulated laughter. An important part of this step is for group members to make eye contact with one another. Dr. Kataria explained, "With a little bit of playfulness it becomes real laughter." And the laughter is contagious.

Most group members said that at first it felt strange to laugh for no reason. But they got used to it, and they like Dr. Kataria's methods. The laughter yoga movement has spread quickly. There are now over 5,000 laughter clubs in 40 countries around the world.

4 **Reread the article in Exercise 3. Circle three examples of direct speech and underline two examples of indirect speech. Then rewrite the sentences with direct speech as indirect speech.**

1. _____

2. _____

3. _____

5 Rewrite each quotation in indirect speech.

1. One woman reported, "I've never laughed so hard in my life!"

   _____

2. A laughter yoga teacher advised me, "Let go of your inhibitions."

   _____

3. A man admitted, "I was laughing to the point of crying!"

   _____

4. Before his first session, he thought, "I can't make myself laugh in front of other people."

   _____

5. An experienced member warned me, "You might feel a little uncomfortable at first."

   _____

6. After her first meeting, a woman said, "I'll be here again next week."

   _____

7. Some laughter club members claim, "The group has changed our lives."

   _____

8. One doctor said, "I'm recommending laughter yoga to all my patients."

   _____

9. The doctor insisted, "Laughter is good medicine."

   _____

10. He said, "I would join the health club if it didn't cost so much money."

    _____

Laughing out loud for 10 to 15 minutes burns between 10 and 40 calories, depending on a person's body weight. This translates to a potential weight loss of approximately 4.5 pounds (approximately 2 kilograms) a year if you do it every day.

6 Read the conversation in direct speech. Then complete the sentences in indirect speech. Circle the correct words or phrases.

Buck: Have you heard the weather report?
Henry: It's supposed to be cold tomorrow.
Buck: Well, it'll be like every other day this week then.
Henry: Yeah, I'm tired of the cold weather.
Buck: Me, too. I can't wait for spring.

1. Buck asked if Henry **has heard / had heard** the weather report.

2. Henry said it **was / had been** supposed to be cold **the next day / that day**.

3. Buck replied that it **would be / would have been** like every other day **that week / last week**.

4. Henry said that **I am / he was** tired of the cold weather.

5. Buck agreed and said he **didn't wait / couldn't wait** for spring.

7 Look at the comic strip. Complete the characters' conversation in your own way.

Now rewrite the characters' words as indirect speech.

1. _The boy advised the pirate that there was a storm coming._

2. _____

3. _____

4. _____

5. _____

6. _____

LESSON 2

8 Complete the conversation. Circle the correct words.

John:	Hey, I have a new joke. Here goes . . . Which animal should you never trust?
Audrey:	Um, I don't know.
Natalie:	Wait! Don't tell me. Um, . . . OK, I give up.
John:	The cheetah!
Natalie:	Ha! **That went over my head. / I don't get it. / That's too much!** That joke is hilarious.
Audrey:	**That's hysterical. / I don't get it. / That's ridiculous.** Can you explain it?
John:	The word "cheetah" sounds like "cheater." You should never trust a cheater.
Audrey:	Oh. You know, **that's pretty silly / I don't get it / that's too much.** I mean, it's really not that funny.

People are more likely to laugh when they hear other people laughing. Television producers have capitalized on this fact since the 1950s by adding laugh tracks, or recordings of people laughing, to comedy programs. When we hear others laughing, we actually feel that the show is more humorous.

9 Rewrite each question in indirect speech.

1. Ann asked, "Did you think that comedian was funny?"

   _____

2. Sophia asked, "Are you going to the party tonight?"

   _____

3. Tom asked me, "How do you remember all those jokes?"

   _____

4. Maya asked Jake, "How many years have you been working here?"

   _____

5. Steve asked Hanna, "What time are you going swimming tomorrow?"

   _____

10 Complete the summary of each conversation. Use indirect speech.

1. **Pete:** Did you hear the joke about the rude parrot?
   Angela: Yes, I heard it, but I didn't think it was funny.
   Pete asked _if Angela had heard the joke about the rude parrot_ .
   Angela said _that she had heard it, but she hadn't thought it was funny_ .

2. **Mr. Adams:** How will you get to the city tomorrow?
   Mr. Jensen: I'll take the train.
   Mr. Adams asked _____
   Mr. Jensen said _____.

3. **Sara:** How many children do you have?
   Alex: I have two boys.
   Sara asked _____
   Alex said _____.

4. **Stu:** How can you laugh at that childish movie?
   Ben: I actually think it's really funny.
   Stu asked _____
   Ben answered _____.

5. **Maria:** How long have you been taking comedy classes?
   Dan: I've been taking them for two years.
   Maria asked _____
   Dan said _____.

11 Think of a cartoon you've seen or a joke you've heard that made you laugh.
Describe the cartoon or write the joke in your own words.

_____

_____

_____

_____

_____

> "If you're too busy to
> laugh, you're too busy."
>
> —Unknown

12 **Read the article.**

What's so funny?

Want to make people laugh? Then you've got to know what's funny. Here are a few tips to keep in mind if your goal is to tickle some funny bones.

Consider your audience.

Your audience, whether it's your kids in your living room or a paying crowd at an auditorium, must be able to connect with any situation you describe in your jokes. If they can't relate to the joke, or if they don't completely understand it, then it's simply not funny to them. People love jokes that, based on their experience, make them say, "That's so true!" If you have to explain a joke to someone, the person might eventually understand it, but he or she probably won't think it's funny.

This is the reason that many jokes don't translate well into another language. They rely on an understanding of a particular culture. You can translate the words but, without an appreciation for the background, many translated jokes aren't very funny.

Use surprise.

There's a reason that people say, "Stop me if you've heard this one" before telling a joke. If your audience already knows (or can guess) the end of a joke before you tell it, then it's not going to make them laugh. People laugh at the end of a joke because they've been told a story and led toward its ending, (unconsciously) thinking about what will happen next or how it will end. When we hear something that wasn't what we were expecting, we find it funny.

Surprise is part of the reason that you want to learn to tell jokes without laughing. If you laugh, then your listeners expect you to say something funny. If you tell a joke without laughing or smiling, then they're more surprised when you get to the funny part.

Check your timing.

Another important part of humor is timing, or delivering the punch line at the best possible moment. It's often useful to pause before telling the last line of a joke. The reason is that this builds tension. The listener knows the end is coming and is waiting for it. When you finally tell the punch line, the listener feels a sense of relief and is more inclined to laugh.

Now reread the article. Choose the best answer to each question.

1. Which of the following is not included in the article?
   a. an explanation of why people laugh
   b. advice on how to tell a joke
   c. an anecdote about a comic experience

2. What should you keep in mind when choosing an audience for your joke?
   a. that the humor of the joke be easy for someone of any culture to understand
   b. that the audience be able to relate to the situation described in your joke
   c. that the audience be able to understand your explanation, in case they don't get the joke

3. Why do people laugh when they hear the punch line of a joke?

   a. because the ending is unexpected

   b. because they can guess the ending before you say it

   c. because you laugh and smile while telling the joke

4. What is one technique to make a punch line funnier?

   a. speak quickly before the audience can guess the ending

   b. pause before the last line, to build suspense

   c. laugh, to indicate that the funny part is coming

13 **Look at the examples of humor. If you can, explain the intended humor of each item in your own words.**

1. Why do elephants have wrinkled feet?
   Because they tie their shoelaces too tight.

   It's funny because the punch line is a surprise. The audience is expecting a scientific explanation, but instead they get the comic image of an elephant wearing shoes.

2. A woman walked up to a little old man rocking in a chair on his porch.

   "I couldn't help noticing how happy you look," she said. "What's your secret for a long happy life?"

   "I smoke three packs of cigarettes a day," he said. "I also drink ten cups of coffee a day, eat fatty foods, and never exercise."

   "That's amazing," the woman said. "How old are you?"

   "Twenty-six," he said.

   _____

   _____

   _____

3. _____

   _____

   _____

   _____

   _____

4. _____

_____

_____

_____

Many comedians warn against analyzing humor too much. As American author, poet, and humorist E. B. White once said, "Analyzing humor is like dissecting a frog. Few people are interested and the frog dies of it."

LESSON 4

14 **Do you think it's ever okay to tell the following types of jokes? Why or why not?**

1. a dirty joke _____

_____

2. an ethnic joke _____

_____

3. a sexist joke _____

_____

15 **Read about the practical jokes. Write a sentence about each one. Use the phrases in the box or your own words. There may be more than one correct answer.**

be a good sport	be the butt of a joke	cross the line
be in poor taste	can take a joke	play a joke on someone

Matt asked his friend Adam to help him play a practical joke on Tricia, one of his co-workers. One day, as Matt and Tricia were waiting for their bus after work, Matt asked Tricia to keep an eye on his briefcase for a minute while he ran to a nearby newsstand to buy the paper. Then Adam came running by and "stole" the briefcase. When Matt returned, Tricia explained that someone had stolen the briefcase while she was supposedly watching it. Matt acted really angry and told Tricia that the briefcase contained something very valuable which he thought she should be responsible for replacing. Tricia refused to pay for anything.

A few minutes later, Adam returned with the briefcase and the guys explained the joke. Tricia was angry that Adam frightened her and didn't speak to Matt for a week.

1. _Adam and Matt played a joke on Tricia._

Jane called a local pizza delivery place and ordered four large pizzas. She gave the name and address of her friend Mark. When the pizza was delivered to Mark's house, Mark was, of course, surprised and confused. The pizza delivery guy insisted that Mark pay for the pizzas. Finally Mark agreed, but he wasn't happy about it.

The next day Jane called her friend and admitted to sending the pizzas. Mark didn't think the joke was very funny since he'd had to pay for food that he didn't want.

2. _____

Jack glued a coin to the sidewalk near the steps of his apartment. He sat down and watched people walking by stop to try to pick it up. When they realized that the coin was glued down, most people looked around to see if anyone was watching, and they looked a little embarrassed.

3. _____

Sue chose a phone number at random out of a telephone book. Through the course of an evening she called the number every half hour and asked to speak with Brian Carr, using a different voice for each call. Each time the woman who answered the phone insisted that Sue had the wrong phone number. After several calls, the woman began to get really annoyed. A few hours later, Sue's friend Bill called the same number. He explained to the woman that his name was Brian Carr and asked if there were any messages for him.

When the woman realized the calls had been a joke, she couldn't help laughing.

4. _____

Did you find any of these practical jokes funny? Why or why not?

_____

_____

_____

16 **WHAT ABOUT YOU?** Read the quotations. Choose one and summarize its meaning in your own words. Do you agree with the point of view expressed? Explain your answer.

"It is the ability to take a joke, not make one, that proves you have a sense of humor."
—Max Eastman
(American journalist and author)

"Life does not stop being funny when someone dies, any more than it stops being serious when someone laughs."
—George Bernard Shaw
(Irish dramatist and literary critic)

"Humor is a rubber sword — it allows you to make a point without drawing blood."
—Mary Hirsh
(American humorist, author, teacher)

"The human race has one really effective weapon, and that is laughter."
—Mark Twain
(American author and humorist)

_____

_____

_____

17 **WHAT ABOUT YOU?** In your opinion, when does a joke cross the line? Write a short paragraph. Consider some of the ideas below, or use your own. Give at least one example to explain your opinion.

- if it is intended to make someone feel bad
- if it causes damage to personal property
- if the person who is the butt of the joke doesn't laugh

- if it embarrasses someone
- if it offends someone
- if someone gets hurt

GRAMMAR BOOSTER

A Read the short conversations and complete the sentences in indirect speech. Then circle all the nouns, pronouns, and possessives that change from direct speech to indirect speech.

Stan: Stop me if you've heard the joke.

Will: I'll tell you if I know it.

1. Stan said _____ to stop _____ (him) if (Will) _____ had heard _____ the joke.

2. Will answered that (he) _____ would tell _____ (Stan) if (he) _____ knew _____ it.

Maya: When can I expect to receive the finished report?

Ross: Actually, it's on your desk. I left it there earlier.

3. Maya asked when she _____ to receive the finished report.

4. Ross replied that it _____ on her desk. He said he _____ it there earlier.

Kellie: What are you doing this weekend? Is anything interesting going on?

Chris: I don't know. I haven't heard about anything big.

Kellie: Well, give me a call if you want to do something.

5. Kellie asked Chris what he _____ that weekend. She asked if anything interesting _____ on.

6. Chris said he _____. He told Kellie he _____ about anything big.

7. Kellie told Chris _____ her a call if he _____ to do something.

Angie: Will you be able to meet us for dinner?

Grace: I'm not sure. I'll have to check my schedule. I'll call you later to let you know.

8. Angie asked whether she _____ to meet them for dinner.

9. Grace replied that she _____ sure. She said she _____ to check her schedule. She told Angie that she _____ her later to let her know.

Paula: Could you please move your plant? It's blocking my view.

Steve: I'll move it as soon as I finish these reports.

10. Paula asked Steve _____ his plant. She said it _____ her view.

11. Steve replied that he _____ it as soon as he _____ the reports.

B Rewrite each of the following sentences in indirect speech.

1. Jackie asked Beth, "When did you see Barbara?"

_____

2. Seth asked me, "Can you make it to dinner on Tuesday?"

_____

3. The teacher ordered the boy, "Put your books on your desk."

_____

4. John promised her, "You won't be disappointed."

_____

5. Jen told Ben, "Please come to the party at my house on Friday."

_____

6. The patient admitted, "I haven't filled my prescription yet."

_____

7. My mom told me, "Don't put too much sugar in my coffee."

_____

8. Heather asked her sister, "Do you want to go shopping with me?"

_____

9. Steve said, "Don't tell me that joke again."

_____

C **Mark grammatically correct sentences with a checkmark. Mark incorrect sentences with an _X_. Then correct the incorrect sentences.**

☐ **1.** Hana told to her friend that she didn't find the movie funny.

☐ **2.** Larry said that slapstick was his favorite type of humor.

☐ **3.** Tori asked to Joe if he wanted to get something to eat.

☐ **4.** My boss said me that I was getting a raise.

☐ **5.** I told him that was the funniest joke I'd ever heard.

☐ **6.** Donna asked what the weather forecast was.

☐ **7.** Yoshiko told that the party would be on Friday.

D **Complete the sentences with reporting verbs from the list on Student's Book page 136. Use as many different reporting verbs as you can.**

1. The CEO _____ that the company had been sold.

2. The newspaper _____ that the soccer team had won the championship.

3. My dentist _____ that I needed to floss every day.

4. Harry _____ that the show really wasn't that funny.

5. Lori _____ that the play was the best she had ever seen.

6. Luke _____ that he would text me every day.

7. Jason _____ that his sister never had to do any work around the house.

8. Phil _____ that he hadn't made a mistake.

A **PREWRITING: ORDERING EVENTS** Think about a joke or story that you can tell.
You don't have to choose a funny story. It can be something that you've experienced,
or it can be something you've heard about, read, or seen in a movie or on television.
Write a list of the main events that happened. Then make sure the events are in the
correct order.

1. _____

2. _____

3. _____

4. _____

5. _____

B **WRITING** On a separate sheet of paper, write the story, telling what happened
and what people said. Use dialogue. Each time you use the direct speech of a
new speaker, begin a new paragraph.

C **SELF-CHECK**

☐ Did I use direct speech in my story?

☐ Did I punctuate direct speech correctly?

☐ Did I correctly paragraph the dialogue?

Troubles While Traveling

1 Complete the chart. Compare and contrast the different types of transportation. What are the advantages and disadvantages of each? Consider the hassles that you face or can avoid with each type.

Type of transportation	Advantages	Disadvantages
car		
plane		
train		
bus		

2 **WHAT ABOUT YOU?** Answer the questions.

1. Which type(s) of transportation do you usually take when you travel? Why?

_____

_____

2. Which type(s) of transportation do you prefer? Why?

_____

_____

THE TEN BEST AIRPORTS IN THE WORLD*

1. Singapore Changi Airport
2. Incheon International Airport (South Korea)
3. Munich Airport (Germany)
4. Hong Kong International Airport
5. Tokyo International Airport (Japan)
6. Zurich Airport (Switzerland)
7. Central Japan International Airport
8. London Heathrow Airport (Great Britain)
9. Amsterdam Schiphol Airport (Netherlands)
10. Beijing Capital International Airport (China)

*Results based on a 31-question survey that asked travelers to rate issues such as wait times and service, ambience and cleanliness, ease of understanding signs, shopping and dining options, and access to public transportation.

3 Complete each conversation with the correct expression.

I'm drawing a blank	it's a safe bet	we'll cross that bridge when we come to it
I'm off	no sweat	
I'm toast	the way I see it	

1. **A:** Are we doing anything this weekend?
   B: It seems like we are, but _____. I just can't remember what it is.

2. **A:** Oh no. I missed the 3:40 train.
   B: Don't worry. I think _____ there's another one leaving soon.

3. **A:** Which cities should we visit on our trip?
   B: Well, _____, we should try to see as much as we can in two weeks.

4. **A:** If I don't get this report done by the end of the day, _____.
   B: Here, I'll help you.

5. **A:** We got to the boarding gate just in time. What if our luggage doesn't make it?
   B: I guess _____.

6. **A:** Oh no! I left my wallet at home.
   B: Oh, _____. I'll lend you money for dinner.

7. **A:** OK, _____.
   B: Safe travels!

4 Choose the correct verb phrases to complete each statement.

1. If we **had taken / would be taking** the train, we **wouldn't sit / wouldn't be sitting** in traffic right now.

2. If she **hadn't talked / hadn't been talking** on her phone, she would **have been hearing / would have heard** the boarding announcement.

3. If the children **had slept / had been sleeping** better, they **wouldn't be arguing / would argue** so much today.

4. If she **isn't traveling / weren't traveling** outside the country, she **wouldn't need / didn't need** her passport.

5. I **wouldn't be using / wouldn't have been using** my cell phone if the plane **would be taking off / were taking off**.

5 Read each statement. Then complete the unreal conditional sentence. Use at least one continuous verb form in each sentence.

1. Alan: It's too bad they overbooked the flight. I was supposed to fly to Spain tonight.

   If they _hadn't overbooked_ (not overbook) the flight, I _would be flying_ (fly) to Spain tonight.

2. Jules: I'm so glad I sat in this seat. I got to meet Sam.

   If Jules _____ (not sit) in this seat, she _____ (not met) Sam.

3. Cara: I wish I'd used the bathroom before we left! Now I can't find one.

   If Cara _____ (use) the bathroom before she left, she _____ (not look) for one now.

4. Rob: I'm glad I'm not hanging out at home tonight. There's nothing to do but watch TV.

   If Rob _____ (hang out) at home tonight, he _____ (watch) TV.

5. Tim and Marcy: We're glad we're traveling during the week. This train is very crowded on the weekend.

   If we _____ (travel) on the weekend, the train _____ (be) much more crowded.

6. Paulo: I wasn't paying attention when I parked the car. Now it's getting towed!

   If Paulo _____ (pay) attention when he parked the car, it _____ (not get) towed right now.

7. Sara and Jeff: We should have packed some snacks to take on the plane. We really don't like this airline food.

   Sara and Jeff _____ (not eat) the airline food now if they _____ (pack) some snacks.

6 WHAT ABOUT YOU? Complete the unreal conditional sentences. Use continuous verb forms and your own ideas.

1. If I were with my family right now, I _____.

2. If it were the weekend, I _____.

3. If I hadn't decided to study English, I _____.

4. If I could be doing anything I wanted right now, I _____.

7 Put the sentences in order. Write the number on the line.

_____ **Brian:** Thanks so much. I really appreciate it.

_____ **Amy:** What's that?

___1___ **Brian:** Amy, could you do me a favor?

_____ **Amy:** Of course not. I'd be happy to.

_____ **Brian:** I've got a horrendous headache. Would you mind getting me some aspirin?

8 Complete each statement of relief or regret, using <u>if it weren't for</u> or <u>if it hadn't been for</u>.

1. _____ the express bus, we would have missed our flight.

2. I would go for a walk with you _____ my sore ankle.

3. _____ Angie, our travel agent, we might have been waiting overnight for a flight.

4. _____ the icy roads, we wouldn't have had an accident.

5. We would be in the museum by now _____ these long lines.

9 Rewrite each statement of relief or regret, using <u>if it weren't for</u> or <u>if it hadn't been for</u>.

1. Without your help, I never would have passed this class.

_____

2. This would be a perfect flight, except for the uncomfortable seats.

_____

3. Without the confusion at the airport, our bags wouldn't have gotten lost.

_____

4. If we didn't have a scheduling conflict, we would go to your party.

_____

5. We would have gotten lost without that stranger's help.

_____

10 Write a request for a favor for each picture.

1. _____

_____

2. _____

_____

3. _____

_____

4. _____

_____

5. _____

_____

11 Now choose one of the situations from Exercise 10 and write a conversation in which someone asks for a favor and expresses gratitude. Use the Conversation Spotlight on Student's Book page 67 as a model.

_____

_____

_____

_____

_____

_____

_____

_____

12 **Read the interview with an Internet hacker.**

The Public Wi-Fi Blues

DD: This is Donald Dean, your roving reporter, going all over the city to give you information on the things that matter in your life. Thanks for listening. I know one of the things that matters to you is security—for your information, for your money, and for your identity. You may feel pretty safe, but in the first six months of this year, there were 1,860 incidents of hacking reported, exposing 228 million records. And we don't know how many went unreported. Of course, most hacking targets business and industry. But you could be a target, too, if you're not careful.

So, today I'm talking to a hacker! Well, she's not really a hacker. Veronica Tyler is a computer security specialist, a real expert. But if she hadn't learned how hackers get into your personal computer, she couldn't help you keep them out. So, Veronica, thank you for agreeing to talk to me and my listeners.

VT: It's my pleasure, Donald.

DD: We're here at Ground Up coffee shop so that you can show me up close what hackers can do in a place like this. Where do we start?

VT: Well, we already took the first step. When we ordered our coffee, we got the Wi-Fi password. Now, I'm turning on my laptop and this clever but nasty little device.

DD: What's it doing? What's that on your monitor?

VT: Information. I'm intercepting signals from laptops, tablets, and smart phones all over the café. This is really basic hacking, and I can already tell you a lot. For example, I can see what Wi-Fi networks each of these people has joined before. And that means I know a lot about them.

DD: Like what?

VT: The guy in the red baseball cap has recently been to Boston. He was logged in to the Logan International Airport network. He stayed at the Morris Hotel, which is very expensive. If I were a real hacker, I would pay close attention to him. He also likes to play golf and eat at fast food places, which are often wi-fi hotspots. But let's get serious now. One of the most effective hacking techniques involves setting up an evil twin.

DD: What in the world is an evil twin?

VT: On a soap opera, it's a character who is supposed to be the twin brother or sister of one of the regular characters. But while the regular character is good and moral, the twin is evil and dangerous.

DD: Okay. If we were talking about soap operas, I would know exactly what you mean. But we're talking about hacking.

VT: And in hacking, an evil twin is a hidden wireless Internet access point that impersonates a legitimate access point. Hackers use it to get sensitive information, like user names and passwords to various accounts.

DD: How does that work?

VT: Well, when someone tries to log in, they see a list of possible networks, right? The name of this coffee shop's Wi-Fi network is on that list, but it's not the same as the name of the shop. It's just a selection of letters and numbers. Now, people are more comfortable with names than with random letter and number combinations. So, on my access point, I've set up another network called GroundUp. It's now on the list, too. Now I'm going to disrupt service for a moment. Okay. Everybody's Wi-Fi connection has gone off. Let's see what happens when people try to reconnect.

DD: They're connecting to GroundUp! The evil twin! So they don't remember or care that what they originally logged in to, the actual coffee shop network, was not named for the shop at all?

VT: No. They happily log in to the evil twin because it's named GroundUp.

DD: I'm afraid I would, too. That's scary.

VT: So, at this point, I can get into their computers and get anything I want. Their online banking credentials, credit card numbers, even Social Security numbers. If it weren't for my honesty and integrity, I could cause a lot of trouble, even do an identity theft. But I couldn't touch the young woman in the green shirt. Her information is encrypted and I wouldn't be able to break the code.

DD: Fascinating. Well, that's all the time we have, Veronica. Thank you for some great information. And now, this is Donald Dean saying, "See you next time."

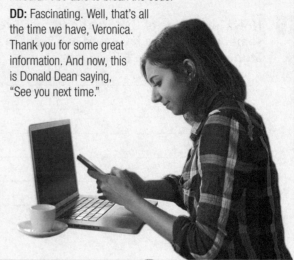

Now answer the questions.

1. What is Veronica Tyler's job? How does she use her hacking skills? _____

   _____

2. What does Tyler's little device allow her to do? _____

3. Why does knowing what Wi-Fi networks people have joined before tell Tyler a lot about them?

   _____

4. Why would a hacker pay close attention to the man in the red baseball cap? _____

   _____

5. What is an evil twin? What does it allow hackers to do? _____

   _____

6. What information *can't* be accessed using the evil twin? _____

7. Before reading this interview, if you were using the Internet, and the Wi-Fi connection were interrupted, do you think you would pay much attention to the name of the network when you logged back in?

   _____

8. Did anything in the interview surprise you? What was it? _____

   _____

13 After reading the interview in Exercise 12, what will you (or should you) do differently the next time you use a public wireless network?

_____

_____

_____

LESSON 4

14 Complete each sentence with the appropriate past participial adjective as a noun modifier.

1. On my last vacation, my luggage was lost. When the airline was unable to locate my

   _____lost_____ luggage, they reimbursed me promptly.

2. A waiter spilled a glass of red wine, staining the front of my dress. I took the the

   _____ dress to the dry cleaners, but they couldn't get the stain out.

3. My son accidentally broke a vase in a souvenir shop. Of course, we had to pay for the

   _____ vase.

4. A thief stole my laptop while I was eating in an outdoor café. Surprisingly, the police caught the thief

   and recovered the _____ laptop within 24 hours.

5. I dropped my new camera and damaged the lens. Luckily, it's still under warranty, so when I called

   customer service they offered to repair or replace the _____ lens.

6. Someone burglarized a suite in the hotel. The police are now searching for evidence in the

   _____ suite.

A Travel Nightmare

Posted: June 6

Let me tell you about my recent travel nightmare. I was flying from Tokyo to Boston for my sister's wedding. I was really busy at work the week before I left, so I didn't really have much time to prepare for my trip. If I had been paying more attention to my preparations, I would probably have had a much better trip. Anyway, the night before my flight I packed in a hurry. I had bought a beautiful new dress for the wedding, and I packed that carefully. But after that, I mostly just threw in clothes, the jewelry that I intended to wear to the wedding, and the wedding gift I had bought for my sister and her husband. Other than that, I'm not even sure what I packed.

The next morning I overslept, so I had to race to the airport and ended up checking in late. Because I was so rushed, I forgot to fill out the identification tag that the airline provided for my suitcase. I didn't even wait at the ticketing counter while they put the destination label on my bag; I had to run to the security checkpoint and barely made it onto my plane before they closed the jetway.

Imagine my dismay when I arrived in Boston, after a tight connection in Los Angeles, to discover that my suitcase hadn't arrived with me! I ended up having to buy a new dress for the wedding, but it wasn't as nice as the one I had packed. And I didn't have the gift that I had packed! My suitcase finally arrived three days later, but by then the wedding was over. I suppose it could have been worse—the gift was undamaged, and my sister loved it—but I could have been dancing without a care in the world at the wedding if I had only taken a few precautions.

Kayo

💬 **Comment**   ➤ **Share**

Now write the things that Kayo did wrong and the things that she should have done.

_____

_____

_____

_____

_____

If you've ever lost your luggage on a trip, then you know it can be a nightmare to recover it. Despite airlines' efforts to reduce the number of lost bags, hundreds of thousands of pieces of luggage still go missing every year, a great deal of which is never reclaimed. What happens to all that stuff? Much of it is bought for a minimal price and resold by a store called the Unclaimed Baggage Center. Each year the store sells millions of items, including suitcases, clothing, cameras, and jewelry, for a fraction of their retail value.

A Read each conditional sentence. Then read each pair of statements that follow. Check <u>True</u> or <u>False</u>.

	True	False
1. If Dave were here, he'd tell us what to do. Dave is here. Dave is going to tell us what to do.	☐ ☐	☐ ☐
2. If she hadn't read the letter, she would have been shocked by the news. She didn't read the letter. She wasn't shocked by the news.	☐ ☐	☐ ☐
3. We might be on the train now if we hadn't gotten stuck in traffic. We're not on the train. We got stuck in traffic.	☐ ☐	☐ ☐
4. If I have time, I may be able to help you out. I am certain that I'll have time. I will definitely help you out.	☐ ☐	☐ ☐
5. If he had taken my advice, he wouldn't be in trouble. He took my advice. He's in trouble.	☐ ☐	☐ ☐

B Choose the correct word or phrase to complete each sentence.

1. If the park gets too full, you _____ wait for some people to leave before they let anyone else in.
   a. had to
   b. wouldn't have had to
   c. have to
   d. didn't have to

2. The air-conditioning automatically turns on if the temperature _____ above 27 degrees Celsius.
   a. goes
   b. will go
   c. would go
   d. would have gone

3. If we had gotten the call earlier, we _____ help.
   a. would
   b. will
   c. were going to
   d. might have been able to

4. Kyle studied very hard for his test. But if he _____, he would be really nervous.
   a. had studied
   b. would have studied
   c. hadn't studied
   d. doesn't study

5. I _____ so excited to go to Paris tomorrow if I had been there before.
   a. wouldn't have been
   b. wouldn't be
   c. won't be
   d. hadn't been

6. If we had time, we _____ the Grand Canyon.
   a. would visit
   b. would have visited
   c. visited
   d. visit

7. I _____ you if you help me first.
   a. helped
   b. will help
   c. had helped
   d. would have helped

8. If Jon _____ on our team, we would have won the game.
- **a.** would have been
- **b.** wouldn't have been
- **c.** had been
- **d.** was

9. Heather _____ surprised right now if you hadn't told her about the party.
- **a.** is
- **b.** had been
- **c.** will be
- **d.** would be

10. If the weather _____ bad, we'll move the party inside.
- **a.** was
- **b.** had been
- **c.** were
- **d.** is

C **WHAT ABOUT YOU? Complete the conditional sentences in your own way.**

1. If I had more free time, _____

_____

2. If we arrive at English class late, _____

_____

3. If I hadn't decided to _____

_____

4. If I spoke English fluently, _____

_____

A **PREWRITING: COMPARE & CONTRAST CHART** Complete the chart below to compare two vacation destinations that you'd like to visit. Write each destination name at the top of the chart. Then fill in the chart with how the destinations are similar and how they are different.

COMPARING VACATION DESTINATIONS

DESTINATION 1: _____

DESTINATION 2: _____

Similarities

_____

_____

_____

Differences

_____ | _____

_____ | _____

_____ | _____

B **WRITING** On a separate sheet of paper, compare and contrast the two places. Use the information in your diagram. Explain which place you think you'd prefer to visit for a vacation. Use expressions of comparison and contrast.

C **SELF-CHECK**

☐ Did I use expressions of comparison and contrast?

☐ Does my essay have an introductory and a concluding paragraph?

☐ Do the supporting paragraphs follow one of the formats illustrated in the Student's Book on page 72?

WRITING MODEL

Two places that I'd love to visit for a vacation are Nice in France and Cinque Terre in Italy. Both are very beautiful places and great vacation destinations. However, there are some differences.

Nice is a busy beach city. There are people from all over the world shopping, eating in world-class restaurants, and going to dance clubs that stay open very late. Similarly, Cinque Terre is also on the water, but the environment is very different. It is still undiscovered by many tourists. In contrast to the fast pace of Nice, most of the visitors to Cinque Terre spend their days hiking, swimming, and visiting olive groves and vineyards.

Both Nice and Cinque Terre are great for vacation. But if I had to choose just one of those places, I think I would choose Cinque Terre. For me, it'd probably be more relaxing.

Mind Over Matter

1 Look at the photos. Which photos show a real situation or event as it actually occurred when the photo was taken? Which photos have been changed using a computer? Are there any that you're not sure about? Write your reactions below.

1. _____

4. _____

2. _____

5. _____

3. _____

6. _____

2 Look back at what you wrote in Exercise 1. Do you think "seeing is believing"? When you see photos online or in newspapers, how do you decide which are "real"?

_____

_____

_____

_____

3 Complete the conversations with expressions from the box.

don't get me wrong	if I were in your shoes	the cat's out of the bag
I may be imagining things	keep in mind	what's on your mind

1. **A:** Can I talk to you for a sec?

   B: Of course. _____?

2. **A:** _____, but I think something's bothering Tina.

   B: Really? _____ that she's really busy at work right now. It might just be that.

3. **A:** I'm trying to decide whether to ask my boss for a raise or not.

   B: _____, I would definitely ask. You deserve one.

4. **A:** Wow, look at this amazing photo!

   B: Hmm. It looks a little fake to me. _____. It's beautiful, but I just think it's been manipulated to make it more colorful.

5. **A:** Gina, is that a new ring you're wearing?

   B: Actually, it is. I was going to make an announcement at dinner, but I guess _____. Jim and I are getting married!

LESSON 1

4 Write <u>a</u>, <u>an</u>, or <u>the</u> before the noun where necessary. Write _X_ if the noun should not have an article. Then write <u>definite</u>, <u>indefinite</u>, <u>unique</u>, or <u>generic</u>.

1. __The__ ingredients in this soup are all organic. ___definite___

2. _____ CEO of our company announced budget cuts. _____

3. _____ Apples are a very popular fruit. _____

4. You should eat _____ apple a day. _____

5. _____ rain is coming down really hard now. _____

6. It's so dry out. Our garden needs _____ rain. _____

7. _____ scam that fooled you also fooled me. _____

5 Complete the sentences. Insert <u>a</u>, <u>an</u>, or <u>the</u> before a noun or noun phrase where necessary. Write X if the noun should not have an article.

1. Phishing is _____ scam designed to steal a person's identity. Victims of _____ scam receive _____ e-mail that appears to come from _____ trusted website such as their bank or favorite shopping site. _____ e-mail attempts to trick people into disclosing valuable personal information like credit card numbers, passwords, or account data.

2. Until the 1800s, British doctors believed that _____ tomatoes were poisonous and caused conditions like "brain fever" and cancer. In fact, _____ tomato is highly nutritious and a good source of vitamin A, which is important for healthy hair and skin.

3. There's _____ new product being marketed on _____ Internet called "Exercise in a Bottle." In pop-up ads, the company claims that _____ product will burn fat while the user is just sitting around doing nothing or even sleeping. _____ ads also state that consumers can enjoy fried chicken, pizza, and other high-calorie, high-fat products and still lose weight.

4. _____ U.S.-based company is in the business of selling stars. For $48 you can purchase _____ star and name it. _____ company has faced a great deal of criticism from _____ astrologers and consumer groups, who point out that the certificates of purchase issued by the company aren't recognized by any other organization. "They can't sell _____ sun because it's not theirs to sell," states one critic of the company.

6 WHAT ABOUT YOU? Describe an ad you've seen that you suspect is a scam. Explain why you don't buy it.

_____

_____

_____

_____

7 Have you ever received an e-mail or phone call that was a scam? Describe the message that you received. What did you do?

_____

_____

_____

_____

8 Read the article. Then choose the best answer to complete each statement.

Aisle or Window Seat? Superstitious or Non-superstitious?

In today's scientific world, many people are reluctant to admit to believing in superstitions. But talk to a few people in the travel industry, and you'll soon learn that superstition is alive and well around the world.

In much of the Western world, it's long been thought that the number 13 is bad luck. Next time you're traveling by air, try looking for row number 13 on your airplane. Chances are, there isn't one. Few airlines have a row 13, and most airlines don't offer flight numbers that contain that number. The airlines offer different reasons for this. One airline spokesperson noted that the taboo associated with the number 13 is an old tradition that has persisted only because it would be too expensive to renumber the rows on hundreds of airplanes.

A spokesperson for a different airline admitted that the airline omits row 13 because too many passengers refuse to sit in those seats. Travel industry studies even show that travel declines on "unlucky" days, such as the thirteenth day of the month.

In parts of Asia, the number 4 is considered unlucky because it has a similar pronunciation to that of the Chinese word for "death." In Japan, the number 9 is avoided because it sounds like the Japanese word for "torture." Some Asian airlines skip these numbers when numbering airplane rows. (Curiously, although the number 13 is not considered unlucky by most Asians, row 13 is also often skipped.) Visit Seoul's Incheon Airport, and you'll notice that there are no gates numbered 4, 13, or 44.

Superstitions about numbers can also be positive. In China, it's said that the number 8 is lucky because

✈	**D E P A R T U R E S**	
Time	**Destination**	**Flight**
19:30	BEIJING	R4 4509
19:30	ATLANTA	EB 7134
19:45	LONDON	DN 0045
19:40	NEW YORK	OD 7158
19:50	FRANKFURT	NP 6890
20:05	DUBAI	UC 1207
20:10	CHICAGO	EB 3436
20:20	TOKYO	R4 4581
20:45	PARIS	NP 1976

its pronunciation is similar to that of the Chinese word that means "to strike it rich." When one airline recently introduced a flight from Beijing to Newark, they named it Flight 88 and offered a "lucky" $888 round-trip ticket price. In the United States, where it is believed that the numbers 7 and 11 bring good fortune, flight numbers containing these numbers are very common for flights to the gambling casinos of Las Vegas.

Superstitious behavior isn't limited to passengers—flight attendants and flight crew have a reputation for being superstitious, too. Some have been known to refuse hotel rooms whose numbers coincided with those of flights that ended in tragedy.

Whether our superstitions are rooted in tradition or personal experience, it seems that most of us pack them up and take them with us, no matter where in the world we travel.

1. The article _____.
   a. offers advice on avoiding bad luck on a trip
   b. recommends that the travel industry change policies that are based on superstitions
   c. explains how superstitions affect the travel industry

2. _____ is considered by many travelers to be unlucky.
   a. A seat in the thirteenth row of an airplane
   b. An airline flight number that contains the number 8
   c. An airport gate numbered 7

3. The article claims that _____.
   a. passengers are more superstitious than flight attendants
   b. Asian travelers are more superstitious than travelers from other parts of the world
   c. some passengers avoid traveling on days of the month that are considered unlucky

4. The article does not claim that _____.
   a. believing in superstitions is old-fashioned
   b. superstitions exist all over the world
   c. some airlines choose lucky flight numbers to increase ticket sales

9 WHAT ABOUT YOU? **Answer the questions.**

1. What numbers are considered lucky or unlucky in your country? Can you explain why?

   _____

   _____

2. Are there any numbers that you personally consider lucky or unlucky? Why or why not?

   _____

   _____

10 **Replace the subject and active verb in each statement with** it **+ a passive reporting verb.**

1. Many people believe that hanging a horseshoe with ends pointing up brings good luck.

   _____ that hanging a horseshoe with ends pointing up brings good luck.

2. They say that picking up a penny on the sidewalk will bring good luck.

   _____ that picking up a penny on the sidewalk will bring good luck.

3. Estimates are that 25% of Americans are superstitious.

   _____ that 25% of Americans are superstitious.

4. People once thought that lightning during a summer storm caused crops to ripen.

   _____ that lightning during a summer storm caused crops to ripen.

5. In some countries, people believe that standing chopsticks upright in a bowl of rice is a symbol of death.

   In some countries, _____ that standing chopsticks upright in a bowl of rice is a symbol of death.

6. People used to say that taking someone's picture was like taking his or her soul.

   _____ that taking someone's picture was like taking his or her soul.

7. People used to believe that a clap of thunder after a funeral meant that the person's soul had reached its final resting place.

8. _____ that a clap of thunder after a funeral meant that the person's soul had reached its final resting place.

11 **What are some superstitions that you know of? Complete the sentences.**

1. In some cultures, it is considered good luck _____.

2. In some cultures, _____ is considered to be bad luck.

3. The numbers _____ are thought to be _____ luck in some countries.

4. An animal that is believed to be good luck in _____ is the _____.

5. If you want your baby to be _____, you should _____.

12 Read the article about visualization as used by elite athletes.

Visualizing the Way to Victory

It's often said that sports are 90 percent mental and 10 percent physical. It may be a cliché, but many athletes and trainers now place a strong emphasis on the mental aspect of training. As many elite athletes will tell you, mental toughness and focus is often the difference that separates the very best (think Olympic gold medal) athletes from the second-best. For almost all elite athletes, visualization, or as some prefer to call it, using imagery, is now a crucial part of their training.

What is visualization? In a nutshell, it involves mentally simulating every aspect of an event, competition, or race. It can be thought of as "athletic training for the brain." Athletes use visualization to build focus, reduce stress, and tune out distractions. While visualization cannot replace physical practice, it can greatly enhance it. Studies have shown that the brain patterns activated when someone visualizes performing a sport are the same brain patterns as those activated by actually doing the sport.

"Visualization might be a misleading term, since using mental imagery involves all five senses," says sports psychologist Dr. Dana Carter. Athletes focus on how things feel, smell, and sound as they go through every moment of their event in their mind. For example, a bobsledder will visualize his or her way down the bobsled track, slowing down the process and "seeing" every inch of the track. "Athletes are actually feeling the ice or the track beneath them, feeling the wind hit their skin, seeing the turns in the track or the moguls on the mountain, hearing their skates on the ice or their body in the water," says Carter. Many athletes even move their bodies as they practice mental imagery because their muscles are responding to the brain signals created as they visualize themselves performing. "It can be a little weird to watch," says Chelsea Yost, an elite skier who has worked with Dr. Carter. "People might be moving their arms, bouncing back and forth, all with their eyes closed and this look of intense concentration on their faces."

Another aspect of mental imagery is known as instructional self-talk. As athletes imagine themselves going through the motions of their event, they tell themselves what to do, step by step—for example, "Point your toes," "Glide, then pull," or "Push off quickly, arms up." Some athletes record this step-by-step instruction aloud, along with what they're seeing and feeling at every moment. They then play it back over and over, feeling muscles in their bodies responding as they would during the actual event. It's believed that mental exercises like this actually train the muscles to respond more quickly.

Yet another aspect of mental imaging is called "pattern-breaking." Pattern-breaking uses imagery to get rid of fear or nervousness. For example, if an athlete has had an accident or been injured while competing, images of the trauma may pop into his or her head before a similar competition. With practice, visualization can help the athlete push out the negative images. Some athletes use an image of a physical action, such as a balloon popping or an elastic band snapping, that they can summon up as a "trigger" to dispel the negative thoughts. Once athletes become adept at pattern-breaking, they are able to banish negative thoughts and maintain positive focus much more easily, which is crucial in competition.

Visualization is not just for elite athletes. Studies have shown that it significantly improves performance in beginning athletes as well. But you need to do more than just think about performing your sport. You need to focus on every little detail: how every moment of the event feels, sounds, looks, smells. Slow down and imagine each step in the event, or in a portion of the event, such as the beginning of a race, or the last hundred yards. You never know—it may give you just the edge over the local competition that you need in your next 5K race!

Now answer the questions.

1. In your own words, what is visualization, or mental imagery? _____
   _____

2. How is it used by athletes? _____
   _____

3. What is instructional self-talk? _____
   _____

4. What effect might instructional self-talk have on the body? _____
   _____

5. What is pattern-breaking? _____
   _____

6. When using pattern-breaking, what images might be used as a "trigger"? _____
   _____

7. How can pattern-breaking be valuable in competition? _____
   _____

8. How is visualization different from just thinking about performing a sport? _____
   _____

13 WHAT ABOUT YOU? Answer the questions.

1. Name a sport or an activity that you do. If you were to try visualization, what details would you need to imagine?
   _____
   _____

2. If you were to try instructional self-talk, what words or phrases might you use?
   _____
   _____

3. In what situations could pattern-breaking help you overcome fear or nervousness?
   _____
   _____

4. What image might you visualize as your trigger to help you banish your fearful thoughts?
   _____
   _____

LESSON 4

14 Complete the conversation between two friends. Use the expressions from the box. Change verb forms and pronouns as necessary.

be all in one's mind	make up one's mind
be out of one's mind	~~put (something) out of one's mind~~
change one's mind	

Kelly: Hey, let's go to a spa on Saturday. We can relax and enjoy ourselves. Let's forget about work and _put it out of our minds_ .
1.

Andrea: That sounds great, but I can't. I'm going to a class. Actually, it's a seminar—to help me get over my fear of dogs.

Kelly: Really? I didn't know you were afraid of dogs.

Andrea: Yeah. I know my fear isn't really logical or real, and it

_____, but I've had trouble getting over it.
2.

Kelly: So what made you decide to try to get over your fear now?

Andrea: Well, it's a little embarrassing. People think I

_____ when I'm terrified of a tiny dog.
3.

Kelly: Everyone's afraid of something.

Andrea: I know, but it's still hard. Everyone in my family loves dogs, and they each have at least one. So I've _____ that I want
4.
to get over my fear so I can go visit them.

Kelly: Well, good luck with the class. And if you _____
5.
about going to the spa, let me know.

15 Read the conversation in Exercise 14 again. Then check <u>True</u> or <u>False</u> for each statement.

	True	False
1. Kelly suggests visiting a spa to relieve work-related stress.	☐	☐
2. Kelly has a phobia.	☐	☐
3. Andrea thinks that her fear of dogs is irrational.	☐	☐
4. Kelly thinks Andrea's fear is crazy and foolish.	☐	☐
5. Andrea has decided to try to overcome her fear.	☐	☐
6. Andrea's fear of dogs is interfering with her life.	☐	☐

16 **WHAT ABOUT YOU?** Answer the questions.

1. List a few things that many people are afraid of. Why do you think people fear these things?

Common fear	Reason
bees	bee stings are painful

2. Do you know anyone who has an irrational phobia? Do you feel sympathy for that person? Why or why not?

_____

_____

3. What advice would you give to someone who wants to get over a phobia?

_____

_____

17 Complete each sentence with the correct word from Student's Book page 83.

1. Kate is an _____. She wouldn't even go near the window of our high-rise apartment.

2. I have _____. I even get scared in elevators unless they're very large.

3. Trey is _____. That's why he won't travel to other countries.

4. Ariana is an _____. She refuses to fly; she always travels by car.

5. Bill must be _____. A little spider landed on him, and he screamed.

6. If you're an _____, don't go in the reptile house at the zoo!

7. Ken prefers small, enclosed spaces. I think he's a little _____.

Glossophobia,
or the fear of public speaking, is believed to be the most common phobia in the world, affecting as many as 75 percent of all people.

A Complete the sentences with <u>a</u> or <u>the</u>. Write ✗ if the noun should not have an article.

1. People in different parts of _____ world have varied superstitions. For example, in some cultures _____ number 13 is considered unlucky, while in others 4 is an unlucky number, and in still others 17 is thought to be _____ bad luck.

2. Bill gave me _____ glass of water to drink. He said that _____ water at his house goes through _____ special filtering system.

3. Lucy bought _____ car last month. _____ car isn't brand new; she bought it from _____ neighbor who had driven it for less than _____ year. But it's in _____ good condition, and Lucy thinks she paid _____ fair price for it.

4. If you're in the mood for Japanese food, I know _____ good restaurant that's not too far from here. _____ restaurant just opened recently, but it's already become one of _____ most popular places in town.

5. _____ success that Jackie has had is because she's _____ hard worker. It has nothing to do with _____ luck.

6. According to _____ recent news program, _____ rich in this country are getting richer, while _____ poor are getting poorer.

B Complete each sentence with a word from the box. Add <u>a</u> if necessary. Each word may be used more than once.

fear	superstition	time	victory

1. I remember _____ when life was simpler. Things were very different then.
2. Deborah Richard's election to the presidency represents _____ for women.
3. There's evidence of interest and belief in _____ in cultures worldwide.
4. Hearing the strange noise, we all felt alarmed and looked at one other with _____.
5. Athletes experience the joys of _____ as well as the pains of defeat.
6. According to _____ that I just recently heard, it's bad luck to walk under a ladder.
7. Neil is afraid of flying. It's _____ he's had since he was a child.
8. Do you have _____ to go get something to eat?

C Rewrite each sentence in the passive voice.

1. The newspaper reported that the politicians were getting close to a deal.

   The politicians _____.

2. They say that tennis player has never lost a match when wearing his lucky tennis shoes.

   That tennis player _____.

3. Most people think my doctor is one of the best in the country.

   My doctor _____.

4. They say that scams affect elderly people far more than the rest of the population.

   Scams _____.

5. In the past, people didn't think the brain had much effect on physical performance.

   In the past, the brain _____.

A PREWRITING: "FREEWRITING" FOR IDEAS

- Choose a fear that you have. On a separate sheet of paper, write for five to ten minutes any words, phrases, statements, or questions about the topic that come to mind.

- Consider exactly what you are afraid of, where the fear came from, how it makes you feel, how it affects your life, and how you might overcome it.

- Write quickly. Do not take time to correct spelling, punctuation, organization, etc.

- Read what you wrote. Circle ideas that go together and add more details.

B WRITING On a separate sheet of paper, describe your fear. Use your freewriting notes for ideas.

C SELF-CHECK

☐ Did I introduce the topic of my fear in general in my first paragraph?

☐ Did all my paragraphs include topic sentences?

☐ Did all my subjects and verbs agree?

WRITING MODEL

I'm afraid of upsetting other people. It's not a fear that actually causes me fright—for me it's more like I feel very nervous about doing something that someone else won't like. This fear probably stems from my childhood when my mother insisted that I always consider how my words and actions would affect other people. Now I rarely do anything without thinking about what other people will think.

This fear is actually a bit annoying because it means that I feel inhibited to do a lot of things that other people do easily. For example, if I receive poor service at a restaurant, I likely won't complain because I think the waiter will get angry with me. I know in my head this doesn't make much sense, but it still feels real for me.

I want to overcome my fear, and I think the way to do that is by doing things that I'm afraid of or anxious about. I think that little by little I might be able to overcome my fear.

Performing at Your Best

1 **Read the tips for improving emotional intelligence.**

Issues
ADHD
Addiction
Anger Management
Anxiety
Child or Adolescent
Depression
Eating Disorders
Relationship Issues
More +

Treatment Orientation
Cognitive Behavioral
(CBT)
Dialectical (DBT)
EMDR
Online Therapy
More +

Video Counseling
See Nearest

Support Groups
Psychiatrists
Treatment Centers

Emotional Intelligence

Sign In | Home |

Would you like to improve your emotional intelligence? Or do you already have a high EQ? No matter where we fall on the emotional intelligence spectrum, most of us could probably benefit from keeping these tips in mind.

1. Follow the old maxim "Think before you speak." Before you tell someone that you're angry about something they've said or done, take a deep breath and count to ten. Chances are you'll calm down enough to find a more positive way to explain your feelings than if you had spoken immediately.

2. Don't take things personally. If your friend said he would text you and he hasn't, it might not have anything to do with you; he might just be busy. Learning to look at situations in a way that isn't centered around yourself can make you calmer and less likely to see things negatively.

3. Practice empathy. This means "putting yourself in someone else's shoes," or imagining the situation from that person's perspective. Often this helps you to understand why other people behave the way they do. Once you understand where people are coming from, it's easier to get along with them.

4. Examine your weaknesses. Be honest with yourself. It's okay to have weaknesses; we all do. Once you know what yours are, you can work on improving them. If you ignore your weaknesses, or worse yet, pretend you don't have any, you'll never have the opportunity to improve.

5. Think about how you react under stress. Do you get more upset than the situation calls for? If so, try some relaxation techniques, such as deep breathing, yoga, or meditation to help you calm down.

Remember: It is possible to improve your EQ. All it takes is a little honesty with yourself and a little work.

Based on the article, write advice for each person.

1. "My assistant came to the meeting without the copies I had asked her to make. They were an important part of my presentation, and I was angry that I wasn't able to hand them out at the meeting. Unfortunately, I yelled at him in front of everyone. I felt bad immediately."

_____

_____

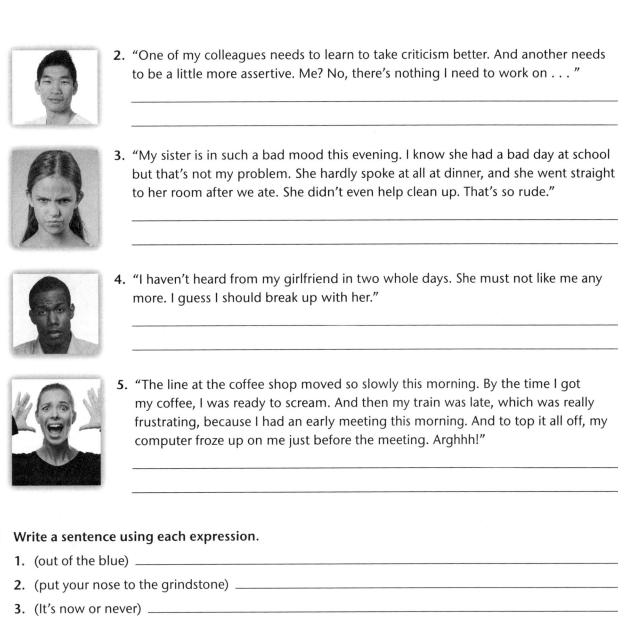

2. "One of my colleagues needs to learn to take criticism better. And another needs to be a little more assertive. Me? No, there's nothing I need to work on . . . "

_____

_____

3. "My sister is in such a bad mood this evening. I know she had a bad day at school but that's not my problem. She hardly spoke at all at dinner, and she went straight to her room after we ate. She didn't even help clean up. That's so rude."

_____

_____

4. "I haven't heard from my girlfriend in two whole days. She must not like me any more. I guess I should break up with her."

_____

_____

5. "The line at the coffee shop moved so slowly this morning. By the time I got my coffee, I was ready to scream. And then my train was late, which was really frustrating, because I had an early meeting this morning. And to top it all off, my computer froze up on me just before the meeting. Arghhh!"

_____

_____

2 Write a sentence using each expression.

1. (out of the blue) _____

2. (put your nose to the grindstone) _____

3. (It's now or never) _____

4. (goes in one ear and out the other) _____

5. (gut feeling) _____

6. (I can't help it) _____

3 What are some of your talents and strengths? Give examples.

_____

_____

_____

_____

4 Read the descriptions of the zodiac signs. Then find your sign. Do you think your strengths and weaknesses match those described? Explain your answer.

_____

_____

Characteristics of the Zodiac Signs

AQUARIUS (January 20–February 18) You are intelligent and inventive. With an independent (and rebellious) mind, you have your own unique way of thinking and refuse to follow the crowd. You have a talent for discovering new ways of doing things. You love electronic gadgets and figuring out how they work. Your unusual lifestyle and unpredictable nature may seem odd to some people.

PISCES (February 19–March 20) You have a vivid imagination and have a talent for writing poetry, creating art, and performing on stage. You care deeply for other people and devote time to helping those who are sick. A daydreamer, you have a habit of seeing life as you want it to be, rather than how it really is. You sometimes allow your emotions to control your behavior.

ARIES (March 21–April 19) You are adventurous and not afraid to try new things. You are always busy and never lazy. You prefer to work independently and don't have patience with people who are slower or less talented. You're not afraid to fight with others to achieve your goals. In your enthusiasm to get things done, you sometimes work too quickly and don't notice smaller points.

TAURUS (April 20–May 20) You have a fondness for luxury and relaxation. You have excellent taste in food, art, and music. After hearing a song just once, you can sing the lyrics or play the melody. Slow to act and speak, you view all sides of a situation before making decisions, and you choose your words carefully. Although some may find you too quiet, you are a loyal friend.

GEMINI (May 21–June 20) A smooth talker, you have the ability to communicate ideas clearly and persuade others to agree with your point of view. Always the life of the party, you have many friends. You are skilled at using tools and fixing machines. Your love of talk sometimes gives you the reputation of being a gossip.

CANCER (June 21–July 22) You are sensitive and emotional. Your love of family is strong, as is your need to protect and care for the people close to you. When making decisions, you have a talent for sensing the correct choice. However, you have a tendency to allow your emotions to get in the way of rational judgments. Shy and easily hurt, you are slow to make friends.

LEO (July 23–August 22) You are a born leader and others naturally look to you for advice and inspiration. An independent spirit, you don't like being told what to do. You love being the center of attention and dislike being ignored. You enjoy playing sports of all kinds, especially in front of an audience. Your desire to be a star sometimes causes you to forget to be a team player.

 VIRGO (August 23–September 22) A perfectionist, you are highly critical of anything that is not done properly. You notice small things that less perceptive people miss. You pick up foreign languages easily. You are highly organized and dislike messiness. With your irresistible urge to improve everything and everyone, you are sometimes seen by others as being fussy and narrow-minded.

 LIBRA (September 23–October 22) Easygoing and charming, you get along with almost everyone. A skilled diplomat, you are good at solving problems and convincing people to compromise. You have a need for peace and avoid conflict and arguments. Because you always see both sides of any issue, you have difficulty making decisions.

 SCORPIO (October 23–November 21) Watchful and perceptive, you quickly sense other people's true thoughts or feelings. You are a good judge of people and a patient listener. However, you are intensely private, and hold back expressing your own emotions. This lack of openness prevents others from getting to know you well.

 SAGITTARIUS (November 22–December 21) Fun-loving and free-spirited, you are happiest when on the move or trying new things. You learn foreign languages easily, and your open-mindedness about other cultures makes travel a rewarding experience. A natural storyteller, you love recounting your adventures, although you often exaggerate the facts. You are easily bored.

 **CAPRICORN (December 22–January 19)** Disciplined and hardworking, you know how to get things done. Determined to succeed, you set goals for yourself and patiently take steps until you achieve them. Shy and cautious with new people, you are often uncomfortable in social situations. You prefer to work independently and have trouble asking others for help.

The head of the Vatican library, Cardinal Giuseppe Mezzofanti (1774–1849), had a real knack for languages. It's believed that when he died at the age of 75, he spoke at least 40 languages fluently. This accomplishment is particularly remarkable considering that the Cardinal never traveled outside of Italy. All his learning came from practice with visitors to the Vatican and from books.

5 Read the statements. Check <u>True</u> or <u>False</u>, according to the information presented in the zodiac descriptions in Exercise 4.

		True	False
1.	Aries signs have an eye for detail.	☐	☐
2.	Taurus signs have an ear for music.	☐	☐
3.	Gemini and Aquarius signs tend to be mechanically inclined.	☐	☐
4.	Pisces signs have a way with words.	☐	☐
5.	Leo, Libra, and Gemini signs have a way with people.	☐	☐
6.	Virgo signs have a head for figures.	☐	☐
7.	Sagittarius signs have a knack for learning languages.	☐	☐
8.	Capricorn signs have a way with people.	☐	☐
9.	Aquarius and Scorpio signs have a good intuitive sense.	☐	☐
10.	Gemini signs are not good with their hands.	☐	☐

6 Read the conversations. Write a sentence about the strengths and/or weaknesses of each person. Use the Vocabulary from Student's Book page 88. There may be more than one correct answer.

Conversation 1

Ray: Thanks again for helping me out with those calculations today.

Diana: No problem. Glad to help.

Ray: You know, I wish I were good at numbers like you.

Diana: Do you? Actually, I'm envious of your talent for learning languages.

Ray: Really? But languages are easy to learn!

Diana: Not for me. I took four years of French and can't even make a sentence!

(Ray) _Ray has a knack for learning languages._

(Diana) _____

Conversation 2

Aidan: Hey, Dave. Nice job on the presentation you gave this afternoon. You got your ideas across really well.

Dave: Thanks. I appreciate that.

Aidan: I could never stand up in front of a big group and give a speech.

Dave: It's not that hard, once you get used to it. It just takes practice.

Aidan: You're probably right, but I think I'll just stick to fixing computers.

Dave: Well, you're really good at that.

(Aidan) _____

(Dave) _____

Conversation 3

Darla: Your scarf is beautiful.

Emily: Thanks. I made it myself.

Darla: You're kidding!

Emily: No. I love doing arts-and-crafts projects.

Darla: Wow, you're so talented. I love the intricate weave.

Emily: Thanks. I can't believe you noticed that. Most people wouldn't pay attention to such a minor part of the design.

(Darla) _____

(Emily) _____

Conversation 4

Andy: Ugh! This stupid watch stopped running again!

Ethan: I can take a look at it if you want. I'm pretty good at fixing things like that. Anyway, I'm sick and tired of studying. I'm never going to remember all these dates for my exam.

Andy: Why don't you make up a song to help you remember them? Put the words to a tune. That's how I usually remember things.

Ethan: That sounds like your area of expertise, not mine. I tell you what: I'll take a look at your watch, and you can help me come up with a song.

(Andy) _____

(Ethan) _____

Conversation 5

Joseph: Congratulations, Barbara. I heard you set another sales record. How do you do it?

Barbara: Honestly, I just seem to know what people want to hear, even without knowing much about them. That makes the sales pitch easy.

Joseph: You make it sound simple, but I could never be a salesperson. Convincing people to buy something just isn't one of my talents.

Barbara: Well, not everyone's a people person.

(Joseph) _____

(Barbara) _____

7 Complete the sentences in your own way. Use <u>do</u> or <u>did</u> for emphasis.

1. I don't have an ear for music. I _do like to listen to it, though._ _____ _____

2. Sam doesn't have a way with words. He _____.

3. Even though we didn't make it to your art show, we _____.

4. I don't usually have a way with people. I _____.

5. Luke doesn't have a knack for learning languages. He _____.

6. _____. I didn't like her mother, though.

8 Mark grammatically correct sentences with a checkmark. Mark incorrect sentences with an *X*. Then correct the incorrect sentences.

1. __*X*__ A psychologist suggested that Kim ~~reduces~~ *reduce* her stress levels.

2. _____ It is agreed that measuring intelligence is very complicated.

3. _____ The company will insist that people will not smoke on company property.

4. _____ I've suggested that she talk to her doctor about ways to stimulate her brain's activity.

5. _____ It's important that you be willing to try new things.

6. _____ If you demand that your daughter doesn't keep secrets from you, she'll want to share things

   with you even less.

7. _____ It's desirable that no one knows the details of the project before it is announced.

8. _____ It's essential that each person remembers his or her role in the process.

9. _____ I feel it's necessary that you be aware of how your actions affect others.

10. _____ They recommended that everyone be sleeping well the night before the test.

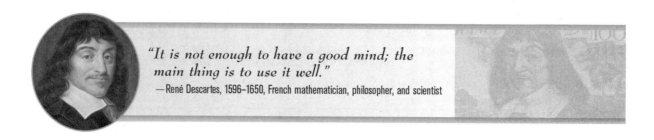

"It is not enough to have a good mind; the main thing is to use it well."
—René Descartes, 1596–1650, French mathematician, philosopher, and scientist

9 Why do you think tests that measure IQ (intelligence quotient) might not be the best way to predict a person's success in work or life?

_____

_____

_____

_____

_____

_____

_____

JOURNAL OF WORLD SCIENCE

"Intelligence" Isn't Universal

In a recent study, Ph.D.s Robert Sternberg and Elena Grigorenko of Yale University evaluated the accuracy of traditional IQ tests in measuring the intelligence of people in non-Western countries. Although these IQ tests have been successful in accurately predicting academic and career success in many Western countries, the study indicated that they may not accurately assess intelligence in other areas of the world. The study suggests that tests devised for Western cultures fail to take into account the different ways that other cultures define and reward intelligence. According to the researchers, if we truly want to measure intelligence, it's essential that we test for different types of intelligence.

The researchers used Sternberg's Triarchic Theory of Human Intelligence to assess aptitudes of children in different cultures. This model identifies three distinct types of intelligence: crystallized, practical, and creative. According to Sternberg's definitions, *crystallized intelligence* refers to academic knowledge and skills. *Practical intelligence* involves the ability to understand and deal with everyday tasks. *Creative intelligence* is a person's ability to react to new situations. According to Sternberg, it's important that we value all three of these types.

Results showed that Kenyan children who demonstrated high practical intelligence performed poorly in areas of crystallized intelligence. The researchers suggest that the reasons for this may lie in Kenyan culture. Some children are kept at home instead of being sent to school. These children, consequently, are more exposed to their indigenous culture. They learn practical skills such as identifying and using medicinal herbs. Since they do not attend school, however, they may feel uncomfortable when placed in a school environment. They score poorly on academic tests of their native language and English. Therefore, standard IQ tests which only assess crystallized intelligence may not accurately test a Kenyan child's full cognitive abilities.

Similarly, the researchers found that in Russia, a country that has recently experienced many social changes, women with high levels of practical intelligence were better able to cope with changing social conditions than other women. If a woman had strong practical abilities, she usually felt more in control of her own life despite the changes going on around her. Even if a woman scored high in crystallized intelligence, this score alone didn't predict life success in this particular culture.

Based on the results of their studies, the researchers advised that we not assume that the cognitive skills valued and useful in one culture are the same as those valued by another. Therefore, they recommend that traditional IQ tests not be the sole method of assessment in non-Western countries.

VOLUME 20, ISSUE 6

Find and underline four places where the subjunctive is used in the article.

11 Complete the sentences with your own ideas. Use the subjunctive.

1. When you feel depressed, I recommend that _____ .

2. If you want to increase your interpersonal intelligence, I suggest
   that _____ .

3. If someone has a hard time talking about feelings, it might be important
   that _____ .

4. A career counselor might recommend that _____ .

12 **WHAT ABOUT YOU?** Read the statements. Do you agree with the opinions
expressed? Write your reaction to each statement.

1. "Even if someone scores very high on IQ and EQ tests, it doesn't prove that the person is very
   intelligent."
   YOU _____

2. "A person is intelligent only if that person has common sense. What good is being able to do math
   problems in your head if you're unable to function in everyday life?"
   YOU _____

3. "Because high IQs and EQs are crucial to success, schools and businesses should use tests to
   measure the intelligence of new students and employees."
   YOU _____

> **The Stanford-Binet scale** is the usual standard by which IQs are measured.
> An average adult IQ score on this scale ranges from 85 to 115. Approximately
> 1 percent of the people in the world have an IQ of 135 or higher (a score
> indicating genius or near genius). According to estimates, which of course are
> an inexact science, Leonardo da Vinci had a staggering IQ of 220!

13 How easy or hard is it for you to focus on a single task for a long period of
time? What makes it hard for you to focus? What helps you focus?

_____
_____
_____
_____

14 Read the article.

GET IN THE ZONE

When athletes are so focused on a task that they are unaware of any physical or mental distractions, they are said to be "in the zone." Athletes know that preparing their bodies for competition is only part of a winning formula; mental preparation is just as important. Getting in the zone means getting into your most productive state.

Corporate competition is similar in many ways to athletic competition. Performing well when the pressure's on is as important for business professionals as it is for athletes. In both fields, success depends on performing better than the competition. Focus and mental preparation are the keys to achievement.

MASTERING THESE EIGHT CONCENTRATION SKILLS WILL ENABLE YOU TO GET IN THE ZONE.

• **Planning:** Although it's important to define long-term goals, there are a lot of steps you need to take in order to make these goals happen. The planning skill involves identifying and updating as necessary the smaller steps you need to take in order to accomplish your bigger dreams.

• **Visualization:** Never underestimate the power of the mind. If you can imagine yourself completing a task, then you'll be successful when you're actually doing it, even if the task may be very difficult or new to you. Envision yourself working toward a goal and overcoming obstacles to achieve it.

• **Mental preparation:** Whether it's a big sales pitch or an important presentation, you need to get your mind ready for the task ahead. Some people find it useful to review their notes right before, while others think about something completely unrelated. Find what works best for you and stick with it.

• **Focusing:** For you to produce your best work, every bit of your energy needs to be channeled into the task at hand. You must train yourself to ignore any thoughts or outside stimuli that may distract you.

• **Staying calm:** Anxiety and nervousness can take your concentration away from the task at hand. Techniques such as deep breathing or taking a short break can help you deal with those unpleasant feelings and get back to doing your best.

• **Positive thinking:** Any time you're working on a task, give yourself positive support and feedback. Take time to note what you're doing well and enjoy the feelings of pride that follow. Use positive thinking to instill confidence in yourself and you can be your own biggest supporter.

• **Boosting your energy:** There are times when you'll feel mentally and physically tired as a result of your work. Successful people learn tricks to give themselves that quick pick-me-up needed to get the job done. Next time your eyes start drooping, try eating a high-energy snack such as crackers with peanut butter or taking a brisk walk around the office.

• **Refocusing:** Disappointment and frustration are a part of life and work, so it's inevitable that sometimes you'll experience these emotions. The trick is to recover from these setbacks quickly and redirect your full attention back to what needs to be done.

Now read about the people. For each person, choose one of the eight concentration skills in the article that you think would be most helpful to that person. Explain your answer. There may be more than one correct answer.

1. "I wish I could learn to be a better public speaker. My new job requires me to give a lot of presentations in front of large groups of people. But I'm really shy and when I get up to make my presentation, I panic. Even if I've spent hours rehearsing my speech, I get nervous and forget everything I wanted to say."
   —*Dave Boyle, London, England*

   Staying calm would help Dave relax when he needs to make a
   presentation. I recommend he try deep breathing or taking a break.

2. "I work really well in the mornings, and I usually get a lot done before lunchtime. But every afternoon at about 3:00, I feel like I'm going to fall asleep at my desk! I'm obviously not too productive when I feel like that."
   —*Jennifer Bowers, Wellington, New Zealand*

3. "I was recently given a task at work that I just can't see myself doing. I mean, me, overseeing an entire project? There are so many steps, and it's so involved. I can't imagine how I'm going to get it done!"
   —*Ana Correa de Costa, Brasilia, Brazil*

4. "I work really hard at my job, and to tell the truth, I'm pretty good at it. But I get down on myself sometimes. If things get difficult or stressful, I tend to focus on what I've done wrong or could have done better—and that just kills my self-confidence."
   —*Pietro di Alberto, Milan, Italy*

15 **WHAT ABOUT YOU?** Answer the questions.

1. Describe a time when you reached your achievement zone. How did you feel?

2. Which of the eight concentration skills mentioned in the article in Exercise 14 do you think are the most effective? Which do you think are the least effective? Explain your answer.

3. Think about the last time you had a deadline to complete a project or to take a test. What techniques helped you stay focused under pressure?

16 Read the article about Shakuntala Devi. Then read the statements. Check <u>True</u>, <u>False</u>, or <u>No information</u>, according to the information in the article.

A Mathematical Genius

"It's a myth that numbers are tough," she said. "They are beautiful; one just has to understand them."

Her name was Shakuntala Devi, but she was often known as the "human calculator." Born in Bangladore, India, in 1933, Devi first astounded her uneducated parents with her calculations at just three years of age. By the time she was six, she was showing off her talents by calculating large numbers in front of university students and professors.

Having received no formal training in mathematics, Devi's abilities have stunned mathematicians. Her now-famous mental multiplication of two 13-digit numbers in 28 seconds earned her recognition in the Guinness Book of World Records in 1980. Aside from multiplication and division of very large numbers, she was able to calculate square and cube roots as well as algorithms in her head. She took only 50 seconds to correctly determine the 23rd root of a 201-digit number. (It took a computer over a minute to complete the calculation.) If given any date in the last century, she could identify the day of the week within seconds.

With no formal education—in her own words, "I do not qualify to even get a typist's job"—Devi inspired students around the world to take an interest in mathematics. "It's a myth that numbers are tough," she said. "They are beautiful; one just has to understand them."

Devi's talents were not limited to numbers. As a child, she taught herself to read and write. She described herself as a voracious reader. And having authored 14 books in English, she became a prolific and perceptive writer. Her books range from children's stories to mathematical puzzles to a cookbook for men.

Unlike some geniuses, Devi was witty and outgoing, giving workshops and interviews around the world. Devi died in 2013, at the age of 83.

	True	False	No information
1. Shakuntala Devi had a head for figures.	☐	☐	☐
2. Devi inherited her talents from her parents.	☐	☐	☐
3. To nurture her special talents, Devi received preferential treatment at school.	☐	☐	☐
4. Devi had only average visual and spatial intelligence.	☐	☐	☐
5. Devi showed signs of genius at a very early age.	☐	☐	☐
6. Devi's intellectual genius was determined by years of formal education and training.	☐	☐	☐
7. Devi was gifted with the ability to write poetry.	☐	☐	☐

WHAT ABOUT YOU? Read the intelligence traits listed in the box. Answer the questions.

curious / inquisitive	perceptive / observant	talented
inventive / imaginative	persistent	witty
open-minded		

1. Which of the intelligence traits do you value in a friend? Explain.

_____

_____

2. Which traits do you value in a colleague? Explain.

_____

_____

3. Are the traits you value in a friend the same as or different from the traits you value in a colleague? Why?

_____

_____

4. Think of someone you believe is very strong in one of the intelligence traits. Give examples to support your opinion.

_____

_____

GRAMMAR BOOSTER

A Write two sentences about each person. Use emphatic stress in the second sentence by adding the auxiliary verb <u>do</u> or by underlining the stressed verb <u>be</u>, the modal, or other auxiliary verb.

1. (Derek) not really very observant / has a way with people
   Derek isn't really very observant. He does have a way with people, though.

2. (Amy) isn't good with her hands / has an ear for music

_____

3. (Gail) doesn't have a knack for learning languages / is talented in other ways

_____

4. (Kyle) doesn't have much confidence / has all the skills he needs to succeed

_____

5. (Victor) doesn't have a lot of experience / has a good intuitive sense

_____

6. (Suri) hasn't found a job yet / is persistent

_____

7. (Tara) hasn't been to Africa / has traveled to many other countries

_____

8. (Travis) doesn't have a teaching certificate / would make a great teacher

_____

B Complete each sentence. Circle the correct word or phrase.

1. If you have time, I suggest **stopping / to stop** for lunch at one of those restaurants.

2. The coach recommends **to get / getting** a good night's sleep before each game.

3. For the team to be successful, it's essential **to work / working** together.

4. Mr. Hammond said it's critical **getting / to get** the package to Shanghai by tomorrow morning.

5. It's urgent for you **to start / starting** the process today.

6. The airline suggests **to arrive / arriving** at the airport check-in counter two hours before an international flight.

C Complete the sentences with the infinitive or gerund forms of the verbs in parentheses.

1. Doctors recommend _____ (exercise) at least three times a week.

2. It's critical that people work _____ (protect) the Earth's environment.

3. I heard that it's necessary _____ (arrive) at the theater two hours before the show starts if you want to get tickets.

4. She advised _____ (seek) help from a local historical society.

5. The teacher suggested _____ (write) an outline to help us organize our ideas.

6. It's important _____ (make) a budget for your personal expenses.

D **WHAT ABOUT YOU?** Complete the sentences in your own way. Use infinitive and gerund phrases.

1. When I was younger, people advised me _____

   _____

2. If a person wants to be healthy, I recommend _____

   _____

3. If a person wants to be successful in life, it's important _____

   _____

"A great victory in my life has been the ability to accept my shortcomings and those of others. I'm a long way from being the human being I'd like to be, but I've decided I'm not so bad after all."
—Audrey Hepburn, actress, model, special ambassador to the United Nations Children's Fund (UNICEF), 1929–1993

A **PREWRITING: BRAINSTORMING IDEAS** Think about your strengths. Choose one and brainstorm ideas. Include ideas on how you got the strength (was it learned or inherited?), its effects on your life, and ways in which you might use it to your advantage in the future.

B **WRITING** On a separate sheet of paper, write about your strength, developing the ideas you came up with through brainstorming in Exercise A. Use the outline below as a guide. Be sure to include connecting words and phrases.

Paragraph 1: State the strength and describe how you think you got that ability.

Paragraph 2: Explain what you have gained as a result of having that strength. Support your ideas with examples.

Paragraph 3: Describe how your strength might help you in the future.

C **SELF-CHECK**

☐ Did my paragraphs follow the outline in Exercise B?

☐ Did I use connecting phrases to focus on causes?

☐ Did I introduce sentences with connecting words or phrases to focus on results?

WRITING MODEL

One of my strengths is my ability to communicate with others. I think I really have a way with people. Because of the fact that my mom is the same way, and I never really had to work at it, I probably inherited the trait.

I think that I have a way with people because they really listen to me. For example, I was class president when I was in high school, and I was able to convince the other student leaders to change their points of view on a few issues. As a result, we made some changes to the school's policies. When I was in college, I had a part-time job at a store in a mall. I learned quickly and was able to teach other workers how to do things. Consequently, I was promoted to manager in less than a year.

My dream job definitely includes working with people. I can't imagine a job where I worked by myself all day. I'm studying right now to become a teacher. I think I'll be a good teacher because I'll be able to use my people skills to connect with students.

What Lies Ahead?

1 Read the advertisements for innovative technologies. Then answer the questions.

Wish you had more time? Add 8 hours to your day!

O. P. Laboratory is currently conducting trials on a new drug that completely eliminates the need for human sleep!

The average person spends one-third of his or her life sleeping. Imagine if you could reclaim all that time by making sleep unnecessary! Just think of all the extra time you'd have available to:

- work extra hours and make more money
- catch up on all those projects around the house
- relax with family and friends
- enjoy hobbies and leisure activities

oplaboratory.com

Under the Sea Development Company

is redefining the idea of "living space."

We're currently developing the world's first underwater city, complete with a school system, a hospital, and a large shopping and entertainment district.

Visit us at undertheseadevelopment.com and learn how we're giving people a whole new idea about the place they call home.

Leave the driving to us!

Himoshi Motors is about to change the way you think about driving forever.

Introducing the world's first auto-pilot car! The AutoCar is self-guided and self-driven. You just input the start and destination locations. Then the AutoCar maps out the route and actually drives you, obeying all traffic signals and relying on sensors that "see" and "hear" other vehicles and respond accordingly.

Interested in seeing the prototype for yourself?

Check out himoshimotors/autocar.com.

Travel through time with your very own Time Machine!

Just imagine being able to:

- go back in time to change the way you handled a situation
- see how your parents really acted when they were young
- give your kids a firsthand history lesson they'll never forget
- look into the future to see the consequence of your choices and decisions

Call today for your free information kit. (800) 555-8460

1. Which invention do you think might catch on easily if it were available today? Why?

_____

_____

2. Which invention, if any, do you think might be available before we know it? Why?

_____

_____

3. Which invention do you think would be most beneficial to people? Why?

_____

_____

4. Which invention do you think might open a can of worms? Explain.

_____

_____

5. Which invention might be a case in which the bad outweighs the good? Explain.

_____

_____

LESSON 1

2   **Read the predictions about future technologies. Circle the passive forms.**

a robot used to find bombs

1. According to some scientists, the need for humans to perform dangerous tasks such as firefighting will be eliminated in the not-so-distant future. These scientists predict that soon robots are going to be relied on to do jobs that could be unsafe for humans. They hope that before too long dangerous work environments will have been made a thing of the past.

a city of the future

2. In 100 years, cities will have been completely redesigned. They will be much more efficient, and renewable energy sources will have been harnessed so that there is almost no pollution. People will be moved quickly and efficiently from one neighborhood to another by non-polluting air taxis. Very tall skyscrapers will be built, with high-speed elevators to whisk residents up and down quickly. Moving sidewalks are even going to be made available for people who don't want to walk.

an employee at work in a home office

3. Within 20 years, the daily commute to work will have been replaced by a short walk from the bedroom to the study. Although face-to-face meetings will still be valued, the majority of people's work will be done in offices in their own home. The need for companies to provide large amounts of office space for employees will be eliminated, and employees won't have to spend time or money to get to their workplace.

3 **WHAT ABOUT YOU?** Which of the predictions in Exercise 2 is most interesting or exciting to you? Why?

_____

_____

_____

4 Complete the sentences. Use the words in parentheses and the passive voice to express the future, the future as seen from the past, or the future perfect. There may be more than one correct answer.

1. Because of an increase in automated jobs, fewer people

   _will be needed_____ (need) by manufacturers in the future.

2. In 1970, a telephone that offered both sound and video was

   developed. Company executives confidently predicted that

   3 million of these Picturephone sets _____ (sell)

   by 1980. However, the Picturephone was a flop.

   the Picturephone

3. Before the next big outbreak of disease, we hope that emergency plans _____ (make)

   and precautions _____ (take) by governments.

4. Experts now say that hydrogen fuel cells _____ (accept) as an alternative source of

   energy within ten to twenty years.

5. By the time the average person can travel into outer space for recreation, many trips

   _____ (make) to all the planets in our solar system.

6. At the turn of the century, few people ever thought that in twenty years the horse

   _____ (replace) by the automobile as the primary means of transportation.

7. In 1961, U.S. president John F. Kennedy made the bold promise that a man _____

   (send) to the moon before the end of the decade.

5 Rewrite the sentences. Change the underlined part of each sentence from the active to passive voice. Include a <u>by</u> phrase if necessary.

1. Within the next fifty years, <u>scientists will introduce technologies that we can't even imagine now</u>.

   Within the next fifty years, technologies that we can't even imagine now will be introduced.

2. By the year 2050, <u>people will have accepted inventions that seem incredible now</u> as a common
   part of life.

   _____

3. I thought <u>a secretary would answer the phone</u>, not the boss.

   _____

4. At this time tomorrow, <u>the courier will have delivered the package</u>.

   _____

5. Because of its global themes, <u>audiences all over the world are going to appreciate the film</u>.

   _____

6. After years of war, <u>government leaders will announce news of the peace treaty</u>.

   _____

6 Make predictions in the passive voice about what will or won't be done in the future. Explain your opinions. Use ideas from the box or your own ideas.

achieve world peace	increase food production
control the weather	protect the environment
discover new energy sources	provide education for all children
establish one international language	reduce costs of medication

1. In my opinion, the costs of medication won't be reduced for a long time. Drug companies are making too much money, and they have a lot of power.

2. _____

_____

3. _____

_____

4. _____

_____

5. _____

_____

LESSON 2

7 Put the conversation in the correct order. Write the number on the line.

_____ Because it's a slippery slope. No one knows how this new technology is going to be applied.

_1_ You know, they say that new technologies are going to totally change the way we live our lives.

_____ True. Sometimes technology develops faster than people can decide how it should be used.

_____ Do you really feel that way? How come?

_____ If you ask me, I think that sounds a little frightening.

8 Match each innovative technology with a possible application. Write the letter on the line.

Technology

1. _____ computer chip implants
2. _____ artificial intelligence
3. _____ genetic engineering
4. _____ cloning
5. _____ remote surgery
6. _____ virtual reality
7. _____ nanotechnology

Application

a. Saving endangered species: Genetic material taken from an animal at risk of extinction could be used to create exact copies of the animal.

b. Long-distance health care: A doctor in a hospital in New York could perform an operation on a patient who is in an operating room in Moscow.

c. Increasing food production: The genes of a plant could be manipulated in a laboratory so that it grows to three times its normal size.

d. Surgery from within: microrobots, or tiny robots, will be able to go inside the human body to perform surgery, making many invasive surgeries unnecessary.

e. A car that drives itself: A built-in computer could take complete control of the car, eliminating the need for a human driver.

f. Combat training: Soldiers can improve their aim and combat skills in a wide range of situations, with no danger to themselves or others.

g. Storing medical records: Medical workers could instantly get a patient's complete medical history just by waving an electronic device over his or her arm.

9 **WHAT ABOUT YOU?** Answer the questions.

1. Choose one of the innovative technologies in Exercise 8 or another technology you know about. What are some possible applications for this technology?

   Technology: _____

   Applications: _____

   _____

2. What are some pros and cons to this type of technology?

Pros	Cons

3. What's your final opinion of the technology? Do the potential benefits outweigh the potential problems? Why or why not?

   _____

   _____

   _____

10 Complete the passive unreal conditional sentences. Use the correct forms of the words in parentheses.

1. Can you imagine having a computer chip put inside your body? According to one company that makes computer chip implants, that reality might not be too far away. The company claims that cases of identify fraud ___*might/would be reduced*___ (reduced) if implants ___*were used*___ (use) for identification.

2. At the present time, human cloning is illegal in this country. But some people argue that it should be allowed. They say that if human cloning _____ (permit), information about how certain illnesses develop _____ (learn) from cloning diseased cells.

3. If the severe side effects of the drug _____ (make) public, patients _____ (warned) about them by their doctors. But the company hid the information, causing many people unnecessary pain and suffering.

4. It seems like the possible future applications of innovative technologies are endless. For example, if the technology _____ (develop) further, computer chip implants _____ (use) instead of keys. Imagine waving your computer-chipped hand at your front door to open it instead of inserting a key to unlock it.

5. A number of soldiers were wounded in an attack far from any hospitals. If remote surgery _____ (use) to treat their injuries, many lives _____ (save).

6. Several non-governmental organizations are working to achieve equal rights for all people. The organizations' supporters say that if equal rights _____ (grant) to all people, opportunities for a new way of life _____ (create) for them.

7. In the past, consumers didn't know a lot about the dangers of certain genetically modified foods, so they were popular. If consumers _____ (inform) about the dangers, then the foods _____ (not buy).

11 Complete the passive unreal conditional statements. Use the correct forms of the words in parentheses and your own ideas.

1. If computer chip implants _____ (use) instead of credit cards, _____
   _____

2. If companies _____ (allow) to clone human beings, _____
   _____

3. If the Internet _____ (not / developed), _____

   _____

4. If the automobile _____ (introduce) sooner, _____

   _____

12 **Complete the sentences with words and phrases from the box. Use correct verb forms where necessary.**

absorb / neutralize	native	unregulated
dramatically	turn things around	

1. The Great Lakes, in the northern part of the U.S., used to be quite polluted, but people

   _____, and now they are much cleaner.

2. Trees and plants _____ carbon, which helps the environment.

3. Development should be planned and supervised by the government. If it is _____,

   the environment will be harmed.

4. Attitudes regarding our environment have changed _____ in the last decades.

5. Sometimes plants and animals that have come from other parts of the world take over and crowd

   out the _____ plants and animals.

Hybrids THE WAVE OF THE FUTURE

Most of us are aware that the cars and trucks that we drive today are powered by a resource that will eventually be used up. Oil, from which we derive gasoline, is a nonrenewable resource, and while experts disagree about how much longer world supplies of it will last, it's inevitable that eventually we'll need to find other ways to power automobiles. Hybrids, or hybrid electric vehicles, provide a practical alternative to traditional gasoline-powered automobiles.

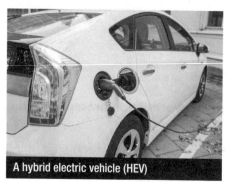
A hybrid electric vehicle (HEV)

The word *hybrid* refers to something that is a mixture of two or more things. Hybrids are automobiles that run on both gasoline and electricity. At low speeds with frequent stops, such as on a city street, the hybrid runs on the more efficient electric motor. To save energy, the engine automatically shuts off when the vehicle comes to a stop, such as at a traffic light, and restarts when the driver puts the car in motion. At the medium or high speeds typical of highway driving, the hybrid operates on its more powerful gasoline engine. The electric motor provides additional power as needed, to help the gasoline engine to increase speed or climb hills. This allows a smaller, more efficient gasoline engine to be used. As a result, hybrids use about half as much gasoline as traditional vehicles.

There are also immediate environmental benefits to driving hybrids. Electricity, unlike gasoline, is a clean energy source that does not release harmful gases into the air. Because hybrids use on average only half as much gasoline as traditional vehicles, they create about half as much pollution. Moreover, the electricity used by hybrids can be generated by renewable resources such as solar and geothermal energy.

If you're still not convinced that hybrids are a good option, then consider the personal advantages to buying this type of vehicle. First of all, hybrids are generally only slightly more expensive than traditional automobiles. With gas prices rising almost daily, imagine the gas in your car lasting you twice as long. You could cut your gas expenses in half. In addition, some governments offer special tax deductions to owners of hybrids or electric vehicles.

Most major carmakers are now producing hybrid options of some of their most popular vehicle models. Based on their growing popularity, it is clear that hybrids are the next big thing in transportation technology.

Choose the best answer to complete each statement.

1. It's important that people reduce their consumption of _____.
   a. geothermal energy
   b. pollution
   c. nonrenewable resources

2. Hybrid vehicles get their power from _____.
   a. waste
   b. solar energy
   c. more than one source

3. Hybrids help protect the environment because _____.
   a. they are powered by nonrenewable resources
   b. they reduce pollution
   c. they are made from recycled materials

4. Vehicles powered by both electricity and gasoline _____.
   a. don't create air pollution
   b. are more efficient
   c. are cheaper to buy than traditional cars

5. Drivers of hybrids have to fill up their gas tanks _____ drivers of traditional vehicles.
   a. more frequently than
   b. twice as often as
   c. half as often as

14 **WHAT ABOUT YOU?** Answer the questions.

Would you consider buying a hybrid car? Do you think that they will become popular in your country? Why or why not?

_____

_____

_____

_____

_____

Recycling one aluminum can saves enough energy to power a TV for three hours. There is no limit to the number of times that aluminum can be recycled. The recycling process doesn't compromise the quality of the metal, so it can be recycled again and again.

15 Look at the graphs. Then read the statements. Check <u>True</u> or <u>False</u>, according to the information.

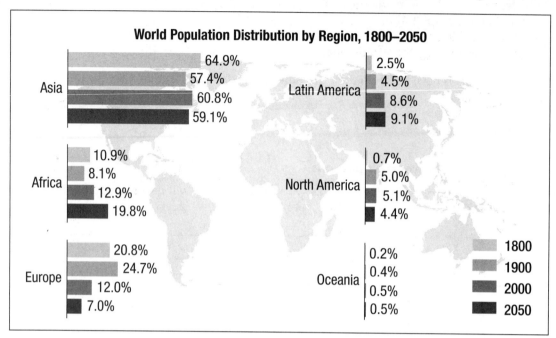

World Population Distribution by Region, 1800–2050

Asia — 64.9%, 57.4%, 60.8%, 59.1%

Latin America — 2.5%, 4.5%, 8.6%, 9.1%

Africa — 10.9%, 8.1%, 12.9%, 19.8%

North America — 0.7%, 5.0%, 5.1%, 4.4%

Europe — 20.8%, 24.7%, 12.0%, 7.0%

Oceania — 0.2%, 0.4%, 0.5%, 0.5%

1800 · 1900 · 2000 · 2050

	True	False
1. The percentage of population increase from 2000 to 2050 is expected to be greater in Africa than the percentage of population increase in Latin America.	☐	☐
2. The largest percentage of the world's population is expected to live in Asia in 2050.	☐	☐
3. Latin America is the only region to show a consistent increase in its percentage of the world's population.	☐	☐
4. North America made the greatest increase in its percentage of the world's population in the last century.	☐	☐

16 Read the article. Then complete each statement, according to the information in the article. Circle the correct word or phrase.

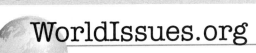

WorldIssues.org

HOME

WHAT'S NEW

POPULATION GROWTH

OTHER GLOBAL ISSUES

RENEWABLE ENERGY

POLLUTION

GENETICALLY-MODIFIED FOOD

MORTALITY RATES

LITERACY RATES

MARRIAGE TRENDS

Population Growth: Four Stages of Development

Population experts studying global population trends have identified four stages that nations experience as they become more developed. In the first stage, both birth and mortality rates are high, so there is little overall growth of the population. Civilization subsisted in this stage for most of human existence, moving into the next stage only within the last 300 years.

In the second stage, improvements in technology and standards of living result in decreasing mortality rates. But the birthrate at this time remains high, so there is a large population growth. Most less-developed Asian and African countries are presently in this stage.

In the third stage, birthrates decrease, resulting in a slower growth rate (if there is any growth at all) in the overall population. This is the case in several European countries, North America, Australia, and Japan, among other places.

A few developed countries, such as Germany and Italy, have now entered the fourth stage of development. In these countries, the fertility rates have dropped so low that mortality rates are actually higher than birthrates, resulting in a decline of overall population.

1. In the first stage of development, birthrates are **low / high** and mortality rates are **low / high**.

2. In the second stage of development, birthrates are **lower than / higher than / the same as** before and mortality rates are **lower / higher / the same**.

3. In the third stage of development, birthrates are **lower than / higher than / the same as** in the second stage. Mortality rates at this time are **lower than / higher than / the same as** in the second stage of development.

4. Canada is in the **first / second / third** stage of development.

5. Birthrates in Germany are **high / low**.

6. A country generally experiences its largest population growth in the **first / second / third / fourth** stage.

> Today it is estimated that 4.3 people are born in the world every second.

GRAMMAR BOOSTER

A Read the following sentences. Write **A** if the sentence is active or **P** if it is passive. Circle the passive verbs.

1. _____ Laws to protect the environment must be passed by the legislature.

2. _____ If the company's policy isn't working, then the managers should change it.

3. _____ The president was interviewed by a famous reporter whose articles have been published in magazines around the world.

4. _____ Citizens must show identification in order to vote.

5. _____ The party will be attended by government officials and other dignitaries.

6. _____ After years of failed attempts, the scientist finally discovered the formula.

7. _____ A number of articles have been written on the topic.

8. _____ First sketches of the designs are made, then samples are constructed.

B Complete each sentence. Circle the correct word or phrase in each pair.

1. My hair **had been cut / had cut** right before that picture **took / was taken**.

2. After the apples **pick / are picked**, workers **wash / are washed** them in cold water.

3. Managers **have reduced / have been reduced** prices on everything in the store.

4. A number of possible solutions **will be discussed / will discuss** at the conference.

5. Caution **should be taken / should take** when storing all household cleaners. Parents **must be kept / must keep** all hazardous materials out of children's reach.

6. The winner **will announce / will be announced** later tonight on a special two-hour program.

C Rewrite each sentence in the passive voice. Include a <u>by</u> phrase if necessary.

1. Researchers have conducted numerous studies on the topic.

   _____

2. First the chef chops onion, basil, and tomatoes. Then he combines all the ingredients.

   _____

3. Patients should take this medication with food to avoid stomach discomfort.

   _____

4. The judges declared Patricia Marks the winner of the country's largest singing contest. They awarded her a check for $100,000 and gave her a new car.

   _____

5. Passengers must provide tickets and identification before boarding.

   _____

6. Members of the health board, who make sure that restaurants meet state health standards, visited The Good Table Café.

   _____

A PREWRITING: PLANNING IDEAS

You will write an essay about life in the future. Choose a topic and write a thesis statement.

Thesis statement:

Possible topics about life in the future:

- New technologies
- New uses for existing technologies
- Future population trends
- The environment
- Your own topic: _____

On a separate sheet of paper, make an outline to plan the supporting paragraphs of your essay. Write a topic sentence for each paragraph you plan to write. Follow each topic sentence with a list of supporting examples.

B WRITING On a separate sheet of paper, write an essay about the topic you chose in Exercise A. Follow your outline. Use your thesis statement and topic sentences. Develop your supporting examples. Don't forget to include an introduction and a conclusion. Refer to the writing model on Student's Book page 108 for an example.

C SELF-CHECK

☐ Does my thesis statement clearly state my argument?

☐ Does each of my supporting paragraphs have a topic sentence that supports my point of view?

☐ Does my conclusion summarize my main points and restate my thesis?

An Interconnected World

1 Read the people's opinions on language and international communication. Then answer the questions in your own way.

①

Menes Beshay, Egypt

I don't see why we need to have an 'international' language. That's what translators are for.

②

Callia Xenos, Greece

I think an international language is a good idea, but I think it should be a created language, like Esperanto, so that no one has the advantage of it being their native tongue.

③

Alfredo Vivas, Chile

Sure, it makes sense to have an international language, but why not make it something other than English? I mean, Mandarin Chinese has nearly three times as many native speakers as English. Why don't we learn that instead?

④

Bianka Gorzowski, Poland

English is the best choice for an international language because it's already been established as the language of business and science. More websites are in English than in any other language, and it's the most popular second language in the world to learn.

1. Which of the opinions above most closely matches your own?

_____

2. Do you think an international language is a good idea? Why or why not?

_____

_____

3. In your opinion, is English a good choice for an international language? Why or why not?

_____

_____

Esperanto is a created language, constructed in the 1870s–1880s by Dr. Ludovic Lazarus Zamenhof of Poland. Zamenhof wanted to come up with a new language that was relatively easy to learn. He hoped that the language would be used internationally as a tool for communication and that it would help to promote global peace and understanding. Although Esperanto has no official status in any country, there are currently 2 million speakers of the language around the world.

2 Complete each conversation with the correct expression from the box.

a fish out of water	how do you like that	money talks	pulling my leg
a losing battle	it's bad enough that	on the fence	

1. **A:** Have you decided which language you're going to study next?

   B: No, I'm still sitting _____. I can't decide between French and Mandarin.

2. **A:** Where's Bill? The meeting was supposed to start 10 minutes ago.

   B: I don't know. I think _____ he called a 7 A.M. meeting, but now he's not even here.

3. **A:** How are you adjusting to your new job?

   B: Honestly? I feel like _____. But I'll get used to it.

4. **A:** Did you hear that Pete made the Olympic team?

   B: What? Are you _____?

   A: No. It's true.

   B: Well, _____!

5. **A:** Do you limit the time your daughter spends on her phone?

   B: I tried to. But it was _____.

6. **A:** Isn't it awful? ComCorp is going to build a factory on the land that was supposed to become a park.

   B: Really? Well, I guess _____.

3 Complete each paragraph. Circle the correct phrasal verbs to complete the sentences.

1. Based on the following fact, many people say that it's time to **bring about / put up with** changes in global education: It would cost $8 billion to provide basic education to every child in the world. There's no reason why any child should have to **go without / lay off** an education.

2. Scientists say that rising ocean temperatures due to global warming will **carry out / wipe out** plankton, the microscopic plants upon which the ocean's food chains are based. If plans are not **put up with / carried out** to stop global warming, all marine life is at risk of extinction.

3. Cholera is a disease of the large intestine. When a person **comes down with / comes up with** the disease, the results can include rapid dehydration and even death. The current cholera epidemic in Africa has lasted for more than 35 years.

4. In the past few years, factory workers in the U.S. have had to **put up with / bring about** declining wages, higher costs for medical benefits, and longer working hours. Now these workers face a new challenge—companies are **carrying out / laying off** employees and moving their factories to less-developed countries where labor is much cheaper.

4 Complete the chart. Make a list of issues that affect the world today. Identify possible problems that these issues could create, and suggest possible solutions. Then answer the questions.

World issues	Possible negative results	Possible solutions
global warming	rising ocean temperatures wipe out marine life	come up with new energy sources to replace those that cause global warming

1. What global issues are you most concerned about? Why?

_____

_____

2. What global issues are you least concerned about? Why?

_____

_____

5 Read the article. Circle the phrasal verbs.

With restaurants in 119 countries, it's clear that McDonald's has become a global brand. And while there are those who criticize the company's expansion and cultural influence, others explain that individual restaurants, most of which are locally owned, modify their menus to (cater to) local diets and tastes.

a McDonald's restaurant in Riyadh, Saudi Arabia

Check out the menus in McDonald's restaurants around the world, and you'll likely come across a surprising number of unfamiliar choices. For example, you can pick up a McFelafel in Egypt, seaweed burgers in Japan, and rabbit in France. Enter a McDonald's in Italy, and you'll find out that you can order an espresso. Wondering about the McAloo Tikki Burger on the McDonald's menu in India? Try it out—but don't count on it including any beef. In India, you'll have to go without a McDonald's signature hamburger, as the chain's restaurants in that country don't serve beef.

6 **WHAT ABOUT YOU?** What's your opinion of large multinational companies like McDonald's? Do you believe that they add to or take away from local cultures and traditions? Explain your answer.

_____

_____

_____

7 Complete the conversations. Circle the correct phrase in each pair. If both phrases are correct, circle them both.

Conversation 1

Jack: This project isn't coming out the way that I imagined it at all. I think we should

(**1. start it over / start over it**).

Ben: I disagree. People are (**2. counting us on / counting on us**) to finish it before the

deadline. We have a good plan. We just need to (**3. carry it out / carry out it**).

Conversation 2

Amy: Have you been to the new Asian fusion restaurant? I'd love to (**4. try it out / try out it**).

Jason: No, actually I haven't. We could go tonight, but we might have to (**5. put up with a crowd**

/ put up a crowd with).

Amy: Hmm. Maybe we should (**6. put off our visit / put our visit off**). A week night might

be better.

Jason: Good idea.

Conversation 3

Iris: You know, I'm really interested in (**7. taking up knitting / taking knitting up**).

Mary: Really? You should do it. I'm sure you could (**8. pick it up / pick up it**) easily.

Iris: You're right. I'd better start looking for a place that offers classes. Is there any chance I can (**9. talk into you / talk you into**) taking them with me?

Mary: Actually, that sounds like fun.

Iris: All right. I'll let you know if I (**10. come anything across / come across anything**).

Mary: Sounds good.

Hooray for . . . Bollywood?

The most popular films in the world do not actually come from Hollywood. Although films from the United States remain very popular worldwide, the Indian filmmaking industry, known as Bollywood, now serves as the primary source of entertainment for more than half of the world's population. While Hollywood releases an average of 475 movies per year, Bollywood is putting out more than three times as many: 1,600 movies per year. According to one BBC poll, the most famous actor in the world isn't an American film star, but Bollywood legend Shah Rukh Khan.

Indian film star Shah Rukh Khan

LESSON 3

8 Complete the sentences with words from the box.

exports	homogenization	investments	prosperity
globalization	infrastructure	outsource	

1. _____ has brought many changes, both good and bad, to the world.

2. When governments make more money from _____ that they send overseas, they are able to invest more money in the _____ needed to support continued growth.

3. Though globalization has increased _____ and the standard of living in many countries, it has also brought many problems.

4. Companies in developed countries _____ many jobs to workers in developing countries.

5. Globalization has resulted in a _____ of culture, some critics say, with many traditions in developing countries being weakened by closer ties to the rest of the world.

6. Shareholders in global companies expect to make money on their _____ in those companies.

9 What changes have you seen in your country due to globalization? Do you see these changes as positive or negative? Why?

_____

_____

_____

10 Read the article.

SWEATSHOPS
The Price of Development?

One of the most publicized results of globalization in recent years has been the transfer of well-paid manufacturing jobs from developed countries to less-developed ones, where workers can be paid much less and goods are significantly cheaper to produce.

Critics of this trend have been vocal. In the developed countries where manufacturing jobs are disappearing, labor protesters claim that the resulting rise in the unemployment rate is hurting the national economy. Critics also point out that when the jobs move to developing countries, the working conditions at many facilities in developing countries are far below the accepted standards in developed countries. At these facilities, commonly known as "sweatshops," employees work long hours, often in dangerous conditions, for low pay. Without government laws against child labor, some workers are as young as five years old.

A typical Western response to sweatshops has been to boycott, or refuse to buy, any imports made under these conditions. Surprisingly, however, opinion polls show that most people in developing countries view these sweatshop jobs positively. Although sweatshop workers in developing nations hope for better wages and working conditions, they don't want consumers in developed nations to protest the situation by refusing to buy the products they make. These boycotts could lead to the closing of factories and employees losing their jobs. Many workers feel that working under these conditions is better than having no job at all.

Moreover, some experts point to statistics showing that sweatshop labor has had a positive economic impact on some developing countries. Average incomes for sweatshop workers are now 5 times what they were less than 20 years ago. The working conditions at some factories have improved, as each company tries to attract the best workers. Decreasing infant mortality rates and rising levels of education are indications of an increased standard of living.

While the pros and cons of sweatshop labor continue to be debated, one fact remains clear —the world economy is rapidly changing into one free-flowing global market. The challenge will be to come up with a way to make globalization work for the benefit of everyone.

Now read each statement. Check <u>True</u> or <u>False</u>, according to the information in the article.

		True	False
1.	The article describes workers moving from developing countries to developed countries in search of jobs.	☐	☐
2.	The number of manufacturing jobs in developed countries is rising.	☐	☐
3.	Factories with poor working conditions are known as "sweatshops."	☐	☐
4.	The article presents arguments both for and against sweatshop labor.	☐	☐
5.	Products that are made by low-paid workers are commonly known as "imports."	☐	☐
6.	Some workers in developing countries have decided to stop buying products made in sweatshops.	☐	☐
7.	Statistics show that wages for sweatshop workers in some countries are rising.	☐	☐
8.	Statistics suggest that sweatshop jobs have increased the level of wealth and comfort in some developing countries.	☐	☐
9.	The article recommends that the globalization of the world economy be stopped.	☐	☐

11 **WHAT ABOUT YOU?** Look at the labels of some things you own. List each item and its country of origin below. Then answer the questions.

Item	Country of origin

1. Do you think it's important to buy products that are made in your own country, rather than to buy goods imported from other countries? Explain your answer.

_____

_____

_____

2. Have you ever participated in a product boycott? Do you think that boycotts can be effective in changing bad company practices? Why or why not?

_____

_____

_____

12   **Read one person's experience with culture shock.**

Veronika Soroková

I have been a student here in the United States for three years. It's almost time for me to return to my home country, Slovakia. I'm excited but also a little sad. It took me a while, but I've grown to love living here in New York City. It wasn't always that way, however.

When I first arrived, I was a bit overwhelmed. Some things were the same as at home, but so much was different! All the new stuff was fun for me for a while. I loved trying new food, like New York pizza and sushi. Then there were the stores—such huge stores, with so many items. It was overwhelming trying to figure out what to buy, but all the choices were also fascinating. There were also so many people from different cultures and countries. That was very different from my hometown, where it was unusual to see someone from another country. I loved just people-watching.

But after a few weeks, I began feeling more overwhelmed and less enchanted. Having so many people around me all the time started to get on my nerves. It didn't help that my English needed some work; I couldn't always understand what people were saying. And of course my lack of fluency in English made my classes a little difficult. I was also having a hard time figuring out what kinds of things were okay to talk about and what were not. For example, I learned the hard way that it's not okay to ask someone how much money he or she makes. At home, that wasn't considered rude. And believe it or not, having all those choices when I went shopping started to get annoying, too. I mean, who wants to choose between fifteen different kinds of toothpaste?

I guess I had come down with a case of homesickness. I missed my family, and I missed hanging out with my friends and being able to communicate easily. Speaking of friends, I was having a hard time making any close friends in New York. My difficulty making friends was in part because I hadn't met the right people, and, in addition, I think I was a little withdrawn and depressed.

Finally though, things started to get better. That was in the spring. I had been here for several months, and my English had improved enough that communicating had become much easier. I made a couple of friends in my classes, and that really helped. One friend was from Japan, and one was actually from New York. She took us to all her favorite places in the city, and I discovered some places of my own, including the Conservatory Gardens in Central Park, which were a perfect place to escape the crowds. But you know what? After a while the crowds didn't bother me like they used to. I guess I had just become part of the crowd myself.

Now write the things that Veronika experienced, positively or negatively, for each stage of culture shock.

Stage 1—honeymoon stage

Stage 2 — frustration stage

Stage 3 — depression stage

Stage 4 — acceptance stage

13 **Answer the questions.**

1. What differences between life in New York and life in her hometown were both positive and negative for Veronika?

   _____

   _____

2. What things about your culture do you think might be negative for a newcomer at first but then might become positive with time?

   _____

   _____

   _____

GRAMMAR BOOSTER

A **Underline the phrasal verbs in each sentence. Then write T if the sentence has a transitive meaning or I if it has an intransitive meaning.**

1. _____ It's a formal event, so everyone should dress up.

2. _____ After hearing the news, the committee called off the celebration.

3. _____ When I think back on those times, they seem like so long ago.

4. _____ The girl grew up in a small fishing village in the north.

5. _____ It's incredibly rude to cut someone off when they're speaking.

6. _____ Please look your essay over before you send it to your teacher.

7. _____ He agreed to go along with the story, but he wasn't happy about it.

8. _____ Please, sit down and make yourself comfortable.

9. _____ The conference was a little boring, but we came away with some good information.

B Read each sentence. Write <u>T</u> if the sentence has a transitive meaning or <u>I</u> if it has an intransitive meaning. Then match each definition to the way the phrasal verb is used in each sentence.

1. _I_ You're being ridiculous. Stop carrying on like that!

2. _T_ We've carried on many of the traditions from when we were children.

3. _____ We blew up balloons to decorate the room for the party.

4. _____ A devoted Tigers fan, John blew up when he heard they had lost the game.

5. _____ I don't want to fight anymore. Let's make up.

6. _____ My grandfather used to make up stories that even the adults loved to hear.

7. _____ Can you turn up the volume on the TV? I can't hear it.

8. _____ After looking everywhere for my keys, they finally turned up under the couch.

continue

behave in a silly way

suddenly become very angry

fill with air

end an argument

create

appear

raise, increase

C Underline the phrasal verbs in each sentence. Then write <u>A</u> if the sentence is active or <u>P</u> if it is passive.

1. _____ The memo was thrown out because we thought it was trash.

2. _____ Someone used up all the hot water before I could take a shower.

3. _____ The poster had to be done over again because the first one was a disaster.

4. _____ They passed out coupons and prizes at the door.

5. _____ That group of kids always leaves Ginny out when they play games.

6. _____ The passengers on the bus were let off at the corner.

7. _____ The application had been filled out with a blue pen.

A **PREWRITING: GENERATING IDEAS**

You are going to write a rebuttal to an opinion or point of view that you disagree with.

- Choose a controversial issue in your city or country that you're concerned about. For ideas, consider current news topics; governmental laws and policies; or social, cultural, and economic issues.

- First, list the opposing point of view. Then list two or three key aspects of that point of view, with your opposing arguments. If you need more space for your notes, use a separate sheet of paper.

Opposing point of view: _____

Key arguments: _____

_____

_____

My rebuttals: _____

_____

_____

Example:

Opposing point of view: *We should not raise taxes on the wealthy*

Key argument: *If the wealthy pay higher taxes, they will spend less, hurting the economy.*

My rebuttal: *The increase in taxes will not be enough to change spending habits.*

B **WRITING** Many publications include a special section for letters they receive from their readers. Writing a "letter to the editor" is one way to express your opinions on issues that concern you. Choose a newspaper or magazine to write to. Write a letter stating a point of view that you oppose and your rebuttal arguments.

C **SELF-CHECK**

☐ Did I summarize the point of view I want to rebut in my introduction?

☐ Did I rebut each argument by providing details and examples to support my own?

☐ Did I use the expressions and transitions or subordinating conjunctions from Student's Book page 120 to link my ideas clearly?

☐ Did I summarize my point of view in my conclusion?